$7\frac{00}{PT}$

A Life
in Stories

Russell
Crowe

A Life
in Stories

Russell Crowe

Gabor H. Wylie

ECW PRESS

The publication of *Russell Crowe: A Life in Stories* has been generously supported by the Canada Council, the Ontario Arts Council, and the Government of Canada through the Book Publishing Industry Development Program. Canadä

CANADIAN CATALOGUING IN PUBLICATION DATA

Russell Crowe: a life in stories
ISBN 1-55022-472-7
1. Crowe, Russell, 1964- . 2. Actors—New Zealand—Biography. I. Title.
PN2287.C76W9 2001   791.43′092   C2001-900737-X

Copyediting by Jennifer Lokash.
Cover by Guylaine Régimbald – SOLO DESIGN.
Typesetting by Yolande Martel.
This book is set in Janson and Amati.

Printed by Transcontinental.

Distributed in Canada by General Distribution Services,
325 Humber College Boulevard, Etobicoke, Ontario M9W 7C3.

Distributed in the United States by LPC Group,
1436 West Randolph Street, Chicago, IL 60607, U.S.A.

Distributed in Europe by Turnaround Publisher Services, Unit 3,
Olympia Trading Estate, Coburg Road, Wood Green, London, N2Z 6T2.

Distributed in Australia and New Zealand by Wakefield Press,
17 Rundle Street (Box 2266), Kent Town, South Australia 5071.

Published by ECW PRESS
Suite 200
2120 Queen Street East
Toronto, Ontario M4E 1E2
Canada.

ecwpress.com

PRINTED AND BOUND IN CANADA

Acknowledgments

It would be criminal not to acknowledge the staggering work of those pioneers (and seemingly tireless pillars) of the burgeoning field of Crowology, the webmasters at "Maximum Russell Crowe." Their site is an amazing testament to their dogged fandom. I thank them for providing an ever-fruitful road stop during my online travels.

I owe many thanks, too, to the gang at ECW Press. You are an appealing group of young people.

Finally, my appreciation goes out to Russell Crowe for having such a storied life. Whatever the virtues or failings of my own work in these pages, let it never be said that my raw material was of anything but the highest grade.

To Angus Rosenberg.
Any size.

Prologue

"Get out of my real life and stick with the fantasy, baby."
—*Russell Crowe, 2000*

Marlon Brando. Robert De Niro. James Dean. Anthony Hopkins. Robert Mitchum. What do these famous men have in common? Depending on which Hollywood observer you ask, they have all found their modern-day incarnation in a certain rarely shaven Australian rancher named Russell Crowe. Now, admittedly, cries of "the next big thing" are sounded so often by the Hollywood marketing machine that one begins to wonder who *isn't* the next Brando or Hepburn, or Dean or Bacall. Even *I* have glimpsed myself in the bathroom mirror, sporting a particularly intriguing or enigmatic facial expression, and wondered, is it . . . could it be . . . *me*? Actually, no, ladies and gentlemen, it is not me. And it is not most of the two-dimensional pretty faces movie marketers would have us believe it is. But if you have picked up this book, it's probably true that you, like me, have a sneaking suspicion that it might just be Russell Crowe.

Crowe's onscreen magnetism and offscreen refusal to pander to the media with grins and long, sugary interviews—"Oh, I'm just a regular guy. No, *really*! I mean, all this is a dream come true, but Hollywood isn't all of me. To tell you the truth, I just love being in nature and having time to myself . . ."—have generated a degree of public curiosity about the man that seems to stand out even among Hollywood's most relentlessly reported-on demigods. Crowe's rugged outback roots, his romantic relationships with the likes of Salma Hayek and Meg Ryan, and his obsessive commitment to his craft have all been investigated extensively (and much to Crowe's chagrin) by information-hungry Tinsel Townwatchers.

But no matter how much Hollywood reporters lust (professionally) and chase (physically) after Russell Crowe, the man remains elusive. He retires to his remote working farm in Australia whenever he can, and for the frenzy of curiosity and trash journalism that does its best to dog him wherever he goes, he has nothing but contempt. When journalist Michael Dwyer once asked him how he could rationalize one thing or another, he snapped, "How do I rationalize having 10 pounds of bullshit written about me on any given day around the globe?" He later said of his public image, "That's got nothing to do with me. That's the thing that Russell Crowe has somehow become and it has nothing to do with me."

Because of Crowe's penchant for privacy (and also because of what I suppose he would call the "several hundreds of pounds of bullshit" that have accumulated around his public persona by now), the writing of this biography has often felt like a massive game of *Where's Waldo?* As it turns out, *Where's Russell?* is much more challenging than its cartoon precursor. The added difficulty of the search for Crowe lies not only in the fact that the actor is rarely to be found sporting a large stripy hat that stands out in a crowd. The real problem arises when the eager biographer actually believes she has *spotted* the target (who may at that moment be, say, scowling at Steve Martin during the Academy Award presentation ceremony or swearing at an incompetent hotel receptionist), and begins to cry happily to readers and fans, "Why, *there's* Russell!" Because before you can say "Maximus Decimus Meridius," everything has changed: Crowe is making charmingly self-deprecating remarks in an interview, sending daily tokens of his affection to the woman in his life, happily riding a Harley along a dusty back-country road in Australia, or dancing with an elderly woman at a bar in Ecuador, moving his hips with the smoothness and necessity of molten lava. In an instant, the brooding superstar evaporates, and the thoughtful, intriguing man materializes.

In short, the search for "the real Russell Crowe" is a difficult—maybe impossible—one. But rather than choosing an angle and running with it, as so many others have done ("He's a monster!" "He's a misunderstood softie!" "He's a genius!" "He's a brutish primadonna!"), I have aimed to create a portrait that reflects the multiplicity I have come to associate with Russell Crowe. For one thing, I have tried to make "the thing that Russell Crowe has somehow become" more my friend than my enemy—a part of the life of Russell Crowe rather than a smokescreen that conceals the man himself.

Russell Crowe: A Life in Stories is Russell Crowe as I have both found him and imagined him, so the episodes in this book are a blend of fact and fiction. Though they are informed by much research on

Crowe's life and work, I have taken liberties with "the straight story" in hopes that I might offer a picture of Russell Crowe that is true in a way that other accounts ("He sleeps with a different woman every night, and he gets into bar fights and sinks his teeth into people's *throats*!") are not. Whether due to gaps in available information or in order to achieve greater immediacy (and, I believe, accuracy), I have followed Crowe's advice and "stuck with the fantasy, baby." Above all, I have tried to have fun reckoning with the man *and* his image. I hope my effort will prove amusing and satisfying to those who are as curious as I was (and still am) about the man who seems more and more like he might just be . . . oh, what the hell: The Next Big Thing.

AS A YOUNG BOY AT SYDNEY BOYS' HIGH SCHOOL ON THE RUGBY TEAM,
FRONT ROW, CENTER

The New Zealand night is barely a fetus, and Russell Crowe isn't much more than seven years old. So far he's evaded the maternal pajama trap he knows is lurking in the house somewhere, but the scent of danger (tooth brushing, face washing, and, worst, of course, bed) is everywhere. He's still dressed and mobile for now, taking in the summer air and a feeling of anticipation which is mostly being generated downstairs, but which is drifting up to him on the second floor through wide-open windows and the off-limits back stairs.

This will be a loud and busy night for his father's pub, which occupies the space twelve feet below Russell's scurrying stocking feet. Although the family moves frequently, they have experienced this general setup more than once: Alex Crowe running a pub downstairs, and his family living in the small apartment overhead.

It's the end of the work week and a gorgeous soft night in mid-summer, and soon every working man and his girlfriend, every wag and joker and loudmouth in town will be arriving to sing, laugh, curse, and drink Red Stripe. Kid Crowe relishes these nights. It's not so much that he can sometimes sneak an extra half-hour of "up time" while the resident authority figures are distracted with cleaning and preparation. It's the *show*.

Russ has pulled a small stool over to the front window of the family's living room and has clambered up to get a better view of the street below. Only a few cars so far. Here's one pulling in: Russ stares as the two passengers step out and wave through the window of the pub to some friends already assembled inside. He doesn't recognize these two. The guy's fresh looking; tight green pants that flare out at the bottoms and a white buttoned-down shirt. The belt buckle looks big and special, but Russ can't make out the details. The lady's in an eggshell yellow dress with a halter neck and some high shoes—she's doing okay at first but stumbles on step four or so. She steadies herself and he pinches her arm and grins. She laughs and smiles at him, then rubs the spot where he pinched her.

Russ scrambles down from the stool, picks it up, races to the other window; sets down the stool, climbs up again for a better vantage point, but just catches the couple's disappearance inside. So much for that pair—except for their unintended (and ungood) farewell: Russ gets a whiff of the man's too-strong cologne as the door swings shut. He grimaces at the odor and then his eyes open wide again. Another car is pulling up. This time four middle-aged guys . . .

Five hours later. Russ has risen from the bed into which he was tucked four and a quarter hours ago. He has lain in wait since the tuck-in, listening attentively to the noise from downstairs and imagining the scenes that might accompany it. His parents are very careful about noise control in the kids' room: thickest carpet possible, closed window, closed door, ear plugs if required. But their efforts are useless on two counts: Terry could sleep through a tidal wave, and Russ, well, here he is now, padding across the small blue room, out into the hallway, and over to his stool by the window. Still plenty of cars outside. At first it seems tonight's wind-down will be a dull one. He can only see two men walking through the patch of light in front of the bar, past the edge of the building toward some parked cars. But then one trips and swears—whatever he says, it's loud and slurred. The other laughs too heartily at his friend's misstep and bellows, "You hold your piss like a lass, mate." The first is incensed by his companion's laughter and fires off a plainly rash remark that Russ can't make out. It's not long before the first drunken punch is thrown, and Russ congratulates himself at least eight times for successfully resisting sleep tonight.

The poorly choreographed boxing match reels on, with much slobbery mockery of mothers and ex-girlfriends, and more "language" than Russ has ever heard uttered at once. He learns no new words tonight, but new combinations abound. After a time, Green Pants emerges from inside and breaks up the scuffle. It takes surprisingly little effort, Russ notes—both featherweights are tired and both are secretly glad to be given a talking-to that lets them go home to bed. With minimal posturing, they lurch off in opposite directions and leave Green Pants to gather up Yellow Dress, who is by now carrying one of her shoes and looking unsteadily and half-heartedly for the other.

"You threw it behind the bar, doll," says Green Pants. "I'll get it for you tomorrow." He opens the passenger-side door and she tumbles in. He walks around to the other side and they motor off.

Russ gets down from the stool. First move: the trip and the sloppy recovery. He does that five times or so. *Quietly*. Not too tough. Drunk, by now, is easy for him to imitate. Thus, Yellow Dress's jerky trip to the passenger seat is a piece of cake. He does it once or twice, but he's got it down before he even tries it. More challenging are Green Pants's peacemaking gestures. Not confrontational (not to rile up the boys when they're on a bit of a tear), instead conciliatory and common-sensical. But firm. *Not* motherly. Russ tries the movements a few times. Can't quite get them. He decides to come back to them and instead tries a few of the happy struts from the arrival period earlier in the evening. Those are easy by now since he's—*Stirring in his mother's room.*

Bare feet down the hall, into his room, door closed, not a sound, into bed.

"Russell and Terry! Boys? Please come in here and help unpack."

Jocelyn Crowe is crouching on the (new) kitchen floor and unpacking a box of kitchenware—plates and other breakables—that she would not let the boys touch if they were clamoring and begging to help, which they are not. She's wondering, though, whether she might be able corral them into the living room where they can help Alex with some of the less fragile items. But then, she doesn't really expect them to come. She always goes through the motions of forcing the boys to participate in the unpacking after the family has moved, but she hasn't the will to enforce the "rule" that the whole family has to help. They move so frequently (she worries that it must be more difficult for the boys than they let on) that she's happy to let them tear around, explore, and get their bearings rather than have them stay inside and put all the Crowe belongings in order *yet again*.

Alex agrees that the Crowes' nomadic lifestyle might be hard on Russell and Terry, but that's not reason enough to cause the family to settle down. The fact is that the boys have far better odds of surviving domestic upheaval than they would of surviving bare cupboards and bare backs, which are the things that all this moving is meant to avoid. Alex goes where there's work—catering work (both Alex and Jocelyn have often worked on movie and television sets providing food for cast and crew), or a pub to run, or whatever else will take him.

The catering is grueling: the mornings are early, and every day requires extensive preparation, but Jocelyn prefers that to running and living over top of pubs. A few years ago, a man was killed in a fight that broke out in a pub Alex was running. "Think of that," Jocelyn still says when the subject of watering hole management comes up, "A man DEAD."

So it is a combination of factors—the fact that movie work is temporary and can dry up quickly, the fact that pubs open and close or become impossible places around which to raise kids, the fact that the family has never had the financial freedom to just settle down and wait out a dry spell. These things have led the Crowes to move (how many times, she pauses to consider) fourteen times in Russell's first ten years.

There is a light scratch at the screen door that enters into an alcove off the kitchen. Jocelyn grunts as she stands up from her work on the floor. She does this hammily, but for no audience in particular, the way tired mothers do as if to say to their children: "*Uh* . . . do you see this? I'm old before my time because you're ungrateful, you urchins." Jocelyn makes her way to the door where a woman wearing a kerchief on her head is peering in, shielding her eyes from the sun to get a better look inside.

"Oh! Hello! I'm Lois. I live next door. Just came over to see who was moving in here."

"We are," Jocelyn says. She introduces herself politely enough as she offers the neighbor her hand, but she doesn't invite the woman in. (She's got a lot of unpacking to do, and she's been trying to swear off neighbors during the past few moves.) Lois has apparently decided that the best way to forge a bond with Jocelyn is to dig into some gossip about the previous tenants here; as she describes the horror of the junk they left lying around, she is trying to peer over Jocelyn's shoulder as subtly as she can.

Jocelyn, meanwhile, over Lois's shoulder, has spotted something else. Russell is standing about five feet behind the new neighbor, partially obscured by a bush. He has his hands folded over his head—these are meant to stand in for Lois's handkerchief—and he is standing on his toes, as if to peek into an area he can't quite see. As he bends and stretches to see the imaginary scene, the corners of his mouth are turned down and his eyebrows are raised; the look signifies extreme curiosity. Jocelyn can't help it: she laughs. Lois turns and catches Russell in his mimicry, and turns back to Jocelyn, suggesting with her eyes that it is Jocelyn's neighborly duty to either severely chastise the boy or at least explain that he has been diagnosed with a condition that prevents him from being polite. Jocelyn is still looking at Russell and, in spite of herself, still chuckling slightly.

"Oh, don't mind Russell," she says, knowing that this explanation is unlikely to do the trick for Lois. "He's just a bit mental, is all." Lois doesn't waste much time before she makes an excuse and departs. Russell and Jocelyn stand staring at each other for a moment; neither is certain whether the shorter of the two is about to be disciplined. "Russell . . ." Jocelyn begins seriously, with the best of intentions. "That was very rude." But it's no good: Russell still has his hands folded on top of his head (not out of insolence, just because he's forgotten to remove them), and Jocelyn breaks into a giggle.

Russell giggles too. Jocelyn turns back toward the kitchen and evaluates her progress with the boxes. Knowing that Russell has already run away, she says only to herself, "Now go help your father."

A gangly, adolescent, and mullet-sporting Russell Crowe is on the floor of his bedroom in his parents' house in New Lynn, folding newsletters and licking envelopes. We're still in the early stages here, thinks the fifteen-year-old, so the print-run is quite small so far. He's produced about twenty newsletters for the members of the Russ le Roq Fan Club—members he feels certain will materialize any day now, as his band Russ le Roq and the Romantics gains exposure and radio play. Russell is the visionary behind the newly formed high school band, and he has no doubt that with a little polish (the polish will consist partly in honing the boys' instrumental and songwriting skills, and partly in cultivating a certain star presence) the group will take off. Many years from now, Crowe will describe the musical style of his grown-up band, Thirty Odd Foot of Grunts (TOFOG to the thoroughly initiated), as largely folk, and will cite Billy Bragg and Tom Waits as influences. For now, his style is more teenage punk than anything, and the possibilities of the genre seem endless.

It's been about a year and a half since Russell underwent the experience that tipped him off to the fact that he was destined to be a musician. He was spending an evening in his family's pub in town; it so happened that on that night, the larger-than-life (or so he

RUSS LE ROQ RELAXING

OCEANIA NEWS AND FEATURES

seemed to the fourteen-year-old) Tom Sharplin was on the bill. It was Crowe's first up-close encounter with what many black jean- and bandana-wearing middle-agers would call "the spirit of rock and roll." The teenager was captivated, desperate to learn guitar; an idol was born in Sharplin and a disciple was born in Crowe. He began a friendship with Sharplin that would endure even as Crowe was catapulted to global celebrity, vastly exceeding both the fame and the fortune of his one-time mentor. (Sharplin will later have a conversation with Crowe that seems to encapsulate the radical shift in Crowe's clout as a performer. Graham Silcock, once a member of Russ le Roq and the Romantics, tells Edmund Davey and Jo Max about Sharplin paying a visit to his music store: "Tom Sharplin came into the shop the other day and mentioned that Russell said he'd like to do a Santana feel for a song. Tom apparently said, 'You want someone who plays like Santana?' Russell replied, 'No, we'll get Carlos Santana.' He was serious. Now he's got the power and the contacts, I guess he can do what he's always dreamed of.")

But all that is yet to come. At the moment, Crowe is on his bedroom floor creating a mail-out for a fan club that doesn't exist. Needless to say, the Russ le Roq Fan Club is a presumption that only an adolescent male ego of the most robust kind could manage. But even now—with pimples, erratic voice, spindly arms, and all— Crowe understands that much of the success of an entertainer depends on the entertainer's perception of himself as such. In an effort to project a rock-star aura (of the most petulant and obnox- ious kind), Crowe and his bandmates have been known to attend performances of other bands at their high school, sitting in the front row only to turn their backs on the performers for the duration of the show. This particular move will ultimately backfire as Russ le Roq and the Romantics will book a show in their own high school auditorium and find themselves performing to an auditorium in which the entire first three rows (full of resentful students returning the insults that Crowe and his cocky sidekicks have paid them and their friends) are facing away from the stage.

As an adult (and as the front man for TOFOG), Crowe will develop more humility, at least about his musicianship. He will remark to Garth Pearce, "I am a virtuoso in my job in that there's not an actor I can't go into a scene with and be absolutely confident that, whatever is required of my character, I can do it. If it had been that way with my music, I would have never gone near acting. But I am a mediocre guitarist and have a so-so singing voice. If I could sit with Eric Clapton, play guitar and get him to give me a little wink, that would be perfect. I know it is not going to happen, because the talent is not there." The wise man knows that if ever he finds himself licking stamps in order to send out a newsletter to the not-yet-signed-up members of his own fan club, it may be a good time to kneel in prayer, thanking the relevant deity for providing him with a day job. And if that day job happens to end up carrying with it Academy Awards and $20-million contracts, the wise man does not complain.

Alex Crowe is fiddling with the sink; it has been a pain for some time, dribbling water incessantly. Most recently, it has begun spraying water in all directions whenever anyone turns on the hot tap. Alex doesn't know exactly how to fix it, but he's doing some preliminary diagnostic work anyway. He should have gotten to it earlier, but somehow not having a job feels much busier and harder than having one. A day that seems entirely empty at the outset—a perfect day for, say, fixing the sink—somehow disappears, whittled away in a sequence of trivial events and tasks, before Alex even realizes it. It's horrifying when you think about it, something Alex is trying not to do. Instead, he has decided to fix the sink.

Jocelyn is out shopping, Terry has just left to meet that skinny girl who's been hanging around lately, and Russell is holding the fridge door open with a bored look on his face—this pose is going on for four minutes or so. "Russ, why don't you climb inside there, close the door, and have a look around. It'll be cheaper." Russell takes out the milk and closes the door, muttering something under his breath—nothing insolent, just making a sound to remind the authority figures of the world that he is eighteen and that these days he is not taking parental nudges lying down.

Truth be known, he's been loitering in the kitchen deliberately. He and his dad are the only ones home, and this seems as good a time as any to initiate The Talk, which he's been thinking about on and off for a while. The key in this discussion will be to seem like a bit of an ass. To seem like a rebellious young man, full of piss and vinegar, ready to throw away his future despite (or in response to) the warnings of the wise. The affectation of the upstart smart-ass persona is the best way to avoid doing any damage at all to his father's pride.

The facts of the case are these: 1) Russell has planned, since early adolescence, to go to university and study history. It's the subject that interests him most at school, and his friends are going to university, and all in all it has seemed like the best plan around for some years; 2) Alex Crowe has been unemployed for almost a year, and there is no money to send Russell to university; 3) Russell has reconciled himself to the impossibility of plan A, and has formulated an alternate plan. The trick is to make this plan sound like, well, like anything other than an unemployment-induced plan B.

"Dad, I've been thinking about next year."

Alex now has his head in the cupboard underneath the sink. He seems to utter a grunt in response to Russell's statement, but the sound may just be a result of the awkward position he's in.

"And I want to—. Well, look. I don't know exactly how it's going to work, but this idea of being an entertainer of some kind . . . it's something I feel I need to pursue. Be it music or acting or whatever. You know?"

Alex worms his way out of the cavity under the sink to look at his son. He looks for a long time. So long, in fact, that Russell has opened his mouth to revive his case by the time Alex finally speaks. "That's not such a bright idea, Russ. You know how many waiters in Sydney . . ."

"... are out-of-work actors? Come on, Dad. Could you find some new artillery? Yeah, lots of actors don't work. But lots do. Especially the good ones. And I'm a good one. Those blokes serving salad in Sydney—well, besides, I'm different because I'll also have a band. I'm diversified, right?" Alex sighs and leans back against the cupboard next to the one he's just been rooting around in.

"Listen, Russ. I'm not going to meddle, son. You and Terry are pretty well men now, and God knows my own dad . . . well, most people don't expect their kids to have the sort of work I've had, with the pubs and the catering for the movie people and that. But this entertainment thing, it's fickle. You can't count on it, Russ. At least go to a technical college or something—get yourself something to fall back on."

Russell laughs loudly. "Dad, I'm pretty sure that at some point in life, hell—maybe again and again, I'll fall on my face. (Can't get any uglier anyway, right?) But I'm also pretty sure I'm never going to fall back, you know what I mean?" Russell grins at his dad, feeling that he has struck a nice balance between willfulness and a genuine appeal for blessing.

Alex looks at his son with an expression on his face that's impossible to read. "Put the milk away," he says as he worms back under the sink.

It's 11 a.m. on a Tuesday, and disgust is rising in Russell Crowe like a freight train full of, well, of all things, steamed milk. He hasn't been working in this cafe long, but he's been here long enough to know the sort of bullshit he's got to put up with—and putting up with things is not this 22 year old's strongest suit. He's struggling these days, working shifts at this trendy "beanery" complete with American tourists and all the dumb chatter one could ask of such a place. He's also busking in the streets of Melbourne, playing guitar and thinking about getting a band together. Anything but "growing up" in the way he's seen others do—artless jellyfish in suits. A nightmare, Crowe thinks. Then again, it has none of the excitement or surreal ache of a nightmare. It's just banality with a healthy dollop of despair on the side. For God's sake: Crowe would rather dress up in fishnet stockings and sing the—but that will come later. For now, he's serving organic herbal tea from Nepal and short dark tall dark double foam—whatever.

He's not used to this kind of place. Years later, he will tell Alex Craig of *HQ Magazine*, "In New Zealand if you asked for a coffee, it was a teaspoon of Nescafe." Here, there's not a jar of instant in sight. The hiss of the steamer, the roar of the grinder, and the endless prattle of these yuppies whose coffees cost more than his haircut are all testament to the utter Nescafe-lessness of this place.

A woman in acid-washed jeans and an off-the-shoulder atrocity on top (folks, it's 1988) sits down at a table by a window. Crowe walks over to her and clicks his pen, pasting on his best (and this particular best is not very good at all) courteous server face. She looks at the chalkboard menu on the facing wall, hesitates sulkily, and finally sighs out her order. As Crowe hears the first strains of Midwest strip mall in her speech, he makes a mental note: Start paying attention to regional differences in U.S. accents.

"Uhhhhm . . . I guess I'll . . . give me a non-fat double latte with extra froth."

Crowe begins to walk away slowly, nodding only once he's turned his back. Then over his shoulder the woman's voice: "Oh, and—God!—make sure it's *decaf*." Crowe, with maximum diplomacy, keeps walking.

After a suspiciously short delay, he returns with a mug. He sets it down in front of the distracted tourist and, for the first time today, smiles in earnest. She looks up at him, wondering why he's still standing there. She tries conspicuously to ignore him as she reaches for her n-f d-l w/ e.f. (decaf.). Before it reaches her mouth, she starts, looks up at the server who hasn't budged, and says with predictable bile, "Ummm . . . hel*lo*. This is just boiling water."

"Lady, when we decaffeinate something in Australia, we don't fuck around."

An hour later, Crowe is seven blocks away smoking a cigarette on a park bench. He chuckles with satisfaction as he opens a free Melbourne daily to finger his way through the want ads.

"And here we go again, ladies and gentlemen; it's a bloody thrilling night for one and all here at Pakatoa Island. Ready? O thirty-four. That's O thirty-four. Everybody got that? Right. B twenty-nine. Dab 'em if you got 'em. B twenty-nine. It's looking good so far, is it, Mrs. Kinsey? Right. N seventeen. [Slight feedback from the sound system.] N seventeen." Russell Crowe, the unlikeliest summer resort bingo caller in the history of summer resort bingo, pauses from his work to take a long swig of something strong from a tumbler.

Russell Crowe is just pulling up his fishnet stockings when someone, he's not sure who, calls helpfully from the corridor outside his shared dressing room, "Hurry up, Russ." Inwardly, in the same cheerful tone, Crowe replies, "Right-o! Fuck off, mate!" He's been playing the same part in the same small theater production in the same town for going on eight months now. He knows his cues, and he knows how long it takes him to get dressed. It is for this reason that it gives him much pleasure to announce (to the riveted audience in his head) that the next person who tells him in a cheerful voice to hurry up will have their arms ripped off and will be summarily beaten about the head with the wet ends of those erstwhile appendages.

Crowe concludes this thought as he is applying red lipstick in a shade called "Dancing Hour." Crowe has come to refer to the color as "Dancing Whore." This is one of the many trivial jokes and games

Russell Crowe

ALL MADE UP FOR *THE ROCKY HORROR PICTURE SHOW*

NEWSPIX

he has developed to keep himself amused as he performs night after night in this same show in this same theater. It's repetitive, but then, it isn't totally deadening either, he thinks as he applies false eyelashes. The show assumes more or less the same form every night, but there are plenty of variables, lots of audience participation, lots to keep the actors on their toes and engaged. Otherwise, Crowe wouldn't be here.

After all, this is not just any old play; it is not even just any old musical. This is *The Rocky Horror Picture Show*, and it is my great pleasure to give you your outrageous, outlandish, and impressively musical host, MR. FRANK N. FURTER. Crowe crams his calloused feet into the leather pumps that await him and takes a few steps to adjust them properly, all the while looking at his gender-bending image in the mirror.

But back to repetition. There have been nights when the play has started to seem dull. Even the campiest show in the world (but wait a minute, *Rocky Horror* is the campiest show in the world) can come to seem banal when one has done it fifty, eighty, two hundred times. (When all is said and done, Crowe will have performed the part of Frank N. Furter four hundred and fifteen times.) Crowe has wondered whether it's time to get out of this gig. It's 1987, he's twenty-four, and he generally avoids ruts and routines like he'd avoid sharing chapstick with Frank N. Furter. He has considered, for example, getting out of acting altogether for a while. He just formed his band, Thirty Odd Foot of Grunts, last year and he could devote more time to that—maybe even do some touring. But more often than not, Crowe decides that the show is still worth doing because he's still learning about improv, still learning how to be light on his feet (pump-clad and aching though they may be).

Crowe has by now made his way to the wings where he awaits his cue. It comes, and Crowe careers onto the stage. A collective whoop comes from the audience; they are thrilled at Crowe's appearance and bearing. Just as Crowe is about to deliver his first line, someone toward the back of the crowd yells, "Nice legs!" The audience appreciates the remark; laughs and scattered applause follow. Crowe camps it up for a moment (showing off the shapely limbs in question) and fires back, "Honey, you'd never make it as a drag queen—the lipstick would never make it 'round your mouth." The audience explodes with laughter.

It is a perfect evening. And the genial light and air leaping off the harbor to meet Russell Crowe's eyes and skin and nose are considerably augmenting his enjoyment of this post-show cigarette. But then again, the post-show cigarette never needs much help in the provision-of-pleasure department. Anyone who has known the satisfaction, slowness, and decadent appropriateness of the post-coital cigarette will also have some appreciation—even if said smoker has never so much as played the triangle in a pit orchestra—of the delight that Russell Crowe is finding in this solitary post-performance smoke. Especially on a night such as this (see above, re: light, air, water) in front of the Opera House in Sydney.

But despite the ambient and incendiary pleasures of the moment, Russell Crowe is not entirely untroubled. "Ah," you will say. "Bad show. Poor Russell." But tonight's was not a bad show. On the contrary, it was an exceptionally good show—even as compared to the string of good shows that always seems to develop in any theater in which Crowe hits the boards on a regular basis. Yes, tonight's was a very, very good show and the trouble nagging Crowe as he rewards himself with this cigarette that so coolly mingles physical pleasure with physical decay is far from self-reproach or even self-doubt.

The problem at the moment is not the show's badness, but precisely its goodness. Crowe finds himself troubled by the fact that said good show—all those deliberate movements, all the lines subtly rendered, all the energy—and not just the energy he personally devoted, but the energy actually generated between cast and audience ("can't be created or destroyed" be damned; sometimes, energy *is* created)—it has all evaporated now. It is lost and will be resuscitated (in a diminished form) only in a review or in an anecdote some theatergoer will tell tomorrow or the next day. In short, the half-life of tonight's charged offering will be about . . . let's see . . . what time is it now?

It occurs to Crowe, as he stubs out the final embers of the cigarette, that although he revels in live performance while he's in the midst of it, the idea that his career as a performer might pass into non-existence so completely, undocumented, unanalyzed (by anyone other than his immediate colleagues and his own tyrannical internal critic), and *unpreserved* is horrifying. On some nights the futility of the project would not be so pungent; Crowe would be capable of telling himself that a character well expressed, an audience truly engaged, in essence, a job well done, is a thing of value no matter how fleeting its life or impact. After all, Crowe has dedicated himself to a life of small battles of integrity and if his victories remain somewhat obscure, then so be it.

But tonight, there is something exceptionally galling about the row of theatrical sandcastles that Crowe can see himself constructing night after night, show after show, only to have them washed away forever by waves of applause and storms of middlebrow journalistic criticism. Tonight there is something horribly self-defeating about the whole endeavor—and it's starting to drive him crazy.

Enter film. Enter the medium by which Crowe has been intrigued since he paddled himself around on his parents' film-set catering carts when he was six years old. Enter frame after frame of meticulously engineered art. Enter jump cuts and deliberate, razor-sharp shadows and extreme close-ups. Enter multiple takes. Enter whispers. *Enter posterity*.

Film, as Crowe sees it tonight, would change everything. ("Of course," he will later joke to Olivier Bonnard, "it also has its inconveniences. The other day, I was saying to Joaquin [Phoenix]: 'You know, I saw *Gladiator* again the other day . . .' And he was looking at me with shiny eyes: 'Yes?' . . . And I said: 'Well . . . you were much better the first time!'") Inconveniences aside, Russell Crowe is at this moment coming to a realization that is going to change his life irrevocably. It won't happen right away; a viable career in film is still a long way off. But when it does happen, it will happen fast. How fast? About 24 frames a second.

Crowe slams down the phone with an indignant bellow: "Piece of fuckin' PISS!" He straightens up and breathes for a second; it's not clear what action will follow the pause. Terry has continued sipping his tea during this outburst. The combination of his quiet good nature and long experience with his volatile and much-loved brother has made the Australian farmer imperturbable. Sudden shouts, things broken, harsh words, even the most soul-searing glares: Terry has stored these up over the years and made of them a suit of tantrum-proof armor that now allows him to respond to his brother's cry without even looking up from the newspaper. "Bit of bad news, mate?"

Russell turns, considers for a minute, then strides like a large, fast cat over to the chair in which his brother is seated. He shoves his unshaven face in front of Terry's and jabs a finger toward his own flawless (and, at the moment, bared) teeth. "See this?" he growls through his clenched jaw. Terry looks. "Yeah."

"And remember when this one—" pointing to a tooth near the front, "was fuckin' elsewhere?"

Terry knows that Russell knows that Terry remembers. "'Course. I was at the match when it got knocked outta your head, mate. You grinned all day, showing off."

"Football," recalls Russell.

"Football."

Russell was only ten when his athletic exertions chiseled a hole in his perfect smile. The two men laugh together, remembering a rambunctious boyhood. Russell's seriousness has vanished as quickly as it appeared. Now he asks, pursuing his case but with less anger and urgency, "And how many jobs have I had since then?"

"Christ, I don't know. You detailed cars for a bit . . . there was the bingo thing," Terry smiles inwardly here, but doesn't dare betray his amusement. "A bit of horse wrangling . . . few months of—"

"*Acting* jobs," Russell barks, irritated by this partial list of his irrelevant bill-paying gigs.

"You've done some plays and that."

"How many films?" Russell turns on his heel.

"Oh. No films, mate, you know that."

Russell paces slowly to the other side of the room and sits down. "Know who that was on the phone?"

Terry feigns ignorance: "What—just now when you were screaming and shouting?"

"Yes. Just now." Russell says this with acid condescension, signaling that he doesn't appreciate his brother's playful evasion.

Terry sighs, deciding that he must submit to this rigged and unavoidable question and answer period. "All right, mate. Who?"

"The fucking movie bloke giving *me* a fucking job," Russell's voice rises to a shout.

Terry is confused. This sounds like good news, but Russell's mood is . . . uncertain, impossible to gauge. He considers a response and comes up with: "Well. Congratulations, then, mate."

A long pause. Russell stares at Terry, who attempts a tricky balance: he stares back to show he's paying attention, but tries to make his eyes a bit dull so the dingo on the loveseat won't mistake his gaze for a challenge. Russell is stonefaced. Only Terry seems to blink.

"Ha!" Russell's sudden shout of laughter is so loud Terry feels it in his own chest. "*Prisoners of the Sun*, it's called. First audition I did after I got the bloody tooth replaced!" Russell roars again with laughter. "Christ—maybe I should get my fucking eyelids done too!" Terry at last feels safe in laughing along. After a minute or so, during which tension drains from the room like cellulite from a Hollywood buttock, Russell wipes a jovial tear from the corner of his eye. He walks over to Terry, slaps him on the shoulder and goes to get his coat. "C'mon, mate," he calls, sticking his head back through the door, "Let's get pissed."

Danielle Spencer would prefer to wait for an appropriate length of time following the mailman's departure. It's a question of dignity, really. Yes, there he is, halfway down the block, concerned with other homes, other letters, bills, and deliveries. But once the postman's location has been deemed sufficiently distant, Spencer immediately whips out to the mailbox like some perfectly evolved wild thing on the Discovery Channel. She pauses before opening the box's small

WITH DANIELLE SPENCER IN 1994

ROY HAVERKAMP / NEWSPIX

metal door, though, reminding herself that there may be nothing at all of interest inside. And that would be fine. Just because the box has contained charming gifts from Russell Crowe, King of Men, every morning for the past four mornings doesn't mean it will contain one today. And if it doesn't happen to contain one today, there is certainly no need to jump to conclusions or become upset or blubber to a sister over the phone or carry on in any way. Or so Spencer tries to tell herself as she stands in front of her mailbox, imagining yet another tiny package with yet another lovely minimalist note from the man she has been dating for—has it been two months already?

Spencer and Crowe met while filming *The Crossing*; they had been nervous because it was a decidedly huge opportunity for both of them. Professionally speaking. They were too busy trying to make their scenes work to even think about one another during the time they were filming. Well, all right, maybe there was time for a thought or two, but not much more than that. Years later, people will ask whether she sensed a glimmer of the five-year relationship to come as she and Russell played out their sex scene together. She might have, she supposes wryly, had she not been preoccupied with her lines, the forty people watching her undress and engage in light foreplay, and—oh yes—the possibility that her whole career could be shattered by an error of any magnitude. Other than those few minor distractions, possible murmurs of romance between her and the leading man were pretty much the only things on her mind.

As it turned out, she and Crowe sensed a mutual attraction by the end of the shoot, and their relationship began soon afterward. She has been pleasantly surprised by Crowe's demeanor during the past several weeks; there has been none of the blustery, demanding persona she saw on the set. Of course, Crowe's seriousness about the film and his willingness to argue and make noise about it never put her off. But she has been amazed at how totally nonexistent those sides of him have been during the time they've spent together since. These deliveries by mail are just one sign of the genuine sweetness she has come to associate with Crowe.

He has been in Melbourne for the past couple of weeks, working on a new project. It's been difficult to be apart so early in the relationship, but work is—has to be—a priority for both of them. Moreover, this has been a useful experiment in that Spencer has found Crowe to be an absolutely top-notch long-distance lover. Take these little deliveries, for instance. Weeks ago, Crowe and Spencer had been in a store together and had come across a fully furnished dollhouse. Spencer had admitted that she was a sucker for such miniature worlds, and had been since she was a little girl. The two had moved on, and Spencer had not thought of it again until this past Monday, when a tiny grand piano had arrived in her mailbox from Melbourne. She had shrieked with delight and amusement, and remarked to herself that it didn't get much sweeter than that. It didn't, until the next day, when the piano *stool* came. Ha! And then a tiny candelabra, and the next day a perfectly crafted rocking chair. Size small, of course.

And so it is that we find Danielle Spencer standing in front of her mailbox (having anxiously awaited the coming, and then the going, of the mailman) wondering what, if anything, Russell Crowe has sent her today. She opens the box and—*yes!*—finds a small package inside. The degree of excitement this package provokes in her is beyond all reason. She politely asks herself to behave like a normal human being for a moment, for the love of God. She does her best to comply with her own request. She races back inside and sits down at the kitchen table. She tears apart the packaging with a savagery that was unknown to her even on childhood Christmases, and soon uncovers a blue plastic capsule. Has he actually found and sent a doll-sized rugby ball? It wouldn't be shocking. She reaches for a small slip of paper that fell out of the package along with the pill-sized object. It reads: *Submerge contents in water. Several hours. —R.* Grinning, she pulls apart the capsule to find an unrecognizable spongy object inside. Realizing that she is about to become extremely late for an appointment, she rushes to fill the sink and submerge the object before dashing out the door.

That afternoon. Danielle Spencer arrives home distracted. She deposits her jacket on a hook by the door and heads for the fridge. On her way, a brightly colored object in the sink catches her eye. She remembers the morning's delivery, and takes two quick steps over to the sink to see what has become of the tiny sponge. It is now a triceratops measuring roughly a foot in length. She begins laughing and does not stop until she has nearly experienced what her mother would call "an accident."

Russell Crowe pulls the laces of his Dr. Martens boot tight below the knee. His army-surplus pants blouse out over the tops of the tall boots, which Russell's friend Dean Cochran has seen and called "shit-kickers." Above the pants hangs a T-shirt which bears a huge, archaic symbol on the front; only some of the people who see Russell Crowe today will know that this symbol was appropriated by Germany's National Socialist party, and has since been reappropriated by neo-Nazi copycats all over the Western world. Partly obscuring the symbol on the T-shirt is a worn jean jacket, which bears its own immediately recognizable symbol: a swastika. Crowe's head is shaven as closely as his face, which at the moment bears an expression that perfectly complements the menacing outfit surrounding it.

Crowe rises from the chair in his bedroom and looks in the mirror: his appearance is startling, he thinks. And perfect. He breathes deeply, trying to fill his clothes out. Of course, he has no trouble filling them out physically; but to occupy these boots and this shirt and this jacket and this haircut—to really live inside them—is a different matter. Crowe stares at his own face in the mirror for five, then ten minutes, breathing, scowling, hardening. Suddenly, he turns on a point and marches out of the room—even while he's still in his own apartment, he takes huge, arrogant strides that are too big for indoors.

Minutes later, Crowe is in public. On the streets of Sydney, he meets as many eyes as he can. He knows people want to stare at him but are trying to look away: he tries to make them look. He tries to make them look at him so he can glare at them, scolding them with his eyes for their audacity. He takes up as much space, physical and psychological, as he can. He tries to force people to walk around him on the sidewalk, take a few steps in the road to avoid his huge striding form that never slows, never acknowledges them, never gives way.

People become silent when they see him. Some shake their heads with averted eyes, some look at their friends with raised eyebrows as if to say, "Do you *see* that guy?" He sees a man with a small son; the son presses his face against his father's hip as Crowe passes. Crowe knows that the man and the boy will soon have a slow conversation in which the boy learns things he has never known before.

Crowe passes a group of teenagers sitting in a doorway who look almost—not quite, but almost—as intimidating as he does. As he moves past the doorway, one of them says, loud enough to be heard, "Nazi prick." Crowe stops as if instantly frozen. He remains in this position for about ten seconds, letting the realization sink in among them: he has heard the insult, and he is not moving on. He turns slowly and approaches the group in two long, slow steps. He bends at the waist to inspect them; the fact that they are seated while he is standing accentuates the power differential between them. He stares down at the group as if they were the Whos down in Whoville and he was some horrible exaggeration of the Grinch. He looks at the one he thinks uttered the insult and opens his eyes wider, as if his hostility has so saturated his body that it is beginning to force his very eyelids apart. At first, partly on principle and partly to avoid the ridicule of his friends, the teenager stares back. It is not long, though, before he averts his eyes, recognizing that this is one of those rare situations that is so damn scary that even a gang of usually merciless adolescent males will let you off the hook if you fold.

Later, in an interview with Amruta Slee, Crowe will describe this experience: "It's a real rush; I can see how it could appeal to you if you didn't have anything else."

Crowe is drawing the line at violence today, so when he has defeated the younger man using only his eyes, he moves on, raking a long look over the entire group before he goes. The only moment at which Crowe hesitates is this: he is walking near Circular Quay, and makes eye contact with an elderly woman on a sidewalk bench. He looks away, not wanting to harass her with his gaze, but can't help looking again, trying to soften his look, hint to her alone that this is just a role, just research, just a game. He knows that it's impossible for his look to convince a stranger forty feet away that this outfit is just a costume and that he doesn't believe in what it represents. But he looks again anyway. The old woman just keeps staring at him with the deep regret of those who are struck, as they near death, by the amazing capacity of things to not improve. Crowe thinks of his grandfather, who photographed the Second World War, who wouldn't even wear his war medals because he believed they stood for destruction. Crowe looks down at himself; he's done his research. He needs to go home.

It's not often that Russell Crowe will refer to a moment, in his
own mind, as "delicious." But there is just no other way to describe
the humor and irony and general delight that are converging right
now on this downtown movie theater in Sydney. Crowe is sitting in
the back row of the cinema, watching the audience file in. Some are
average moviegoers: middle-aged couples unconsciously wearing
clothing that has, over years of marriage, begun to match; elderly
people by themselves who never buy refreshments; a few gay
couples, starved for representations of themselves on the big screen,
who have obviously heard some advance buzz about the film. Many,
though, are testosterone-charged teenagers with shaven heads and
highly dubious political agendas (if one can call "fuckin' shit up" a
political agenda). They enter the theater loudly, shouting to each
other across long distances, mindless (or, rather, deliberately disre-
spectful) of other patrons' comfort. As they yell and curse and tease
one another and drape themselves across two or three seats each,
they implicitly dare ushers and the other moviegoers to challenge
them, which no one does.

Although under other circumstances Crowe would likely scowl
and refer to the conspicuous jerks as "little arseholes," at the moment
he seems pleased. The more they scatter their social urine around
the theater, proclaiming their dominance in the room, the more
Crowe seems to enjoy them. He has been imagining this moment
since he first decided to accept the role of an unassuming gay
plumber opposite Jack Thompson in *The Sum of Us*. He can't
wait for these guys, who have obviously decided to follow Crowe's

47

career after seeing *Romper Stomper*, to realize what they've bought tickets for.

After *Romper Stomper* was released, Crowe began to develop a strange fan base, one he wanted to alienate as quickly as possible. He could understand how kids like these—like the ones who are now semi-deliberately spilling their popcorn in the laps of those unfortunate enough to be seated beside them—might have read *Romper Stomper* as a glorification of the neo-Nazi gang it depicted. Crowe himself had called Geoffrey Wright before agreeing to make the film and asked point blank: "Listen, mate, are you a Nazi?" Wright wasn't a Nazi and neither, of course, is Crowe.

Crowe took the part because the script had fascinated him—its anger, its brutality, its desperation. He wanted a chance to explore the interplay of Hando and his gang: how a man who is totally defined by his leadership of a group changes (in Hando's case, comes apart) when he is deprived of followers. And Crowe's effort was, by the standards of his profession, successful. He won the 1992 Australian Film Institute award for best male performance. But what worked in dramatic terms was problematic in political terms. Crowe quickly became a minor icon among racist and right wing extremist elements in Australia. Either they assumed that Crowe's willingness to play Hando signaled the actor's approval of the character's behavior and ideology, or they just couldn't grasp the division between the fantasy of the film and the gritty world it depicted. Crowe was bothered by this new cult popularity. Not only was it personally upsetting, but he also feared it would hurt his career.

So when he was offered the part in *The Sum of Us*, he took it. There's not much that can purge your reputation of any and all suggestions of Nazi sympathies, Crowe figured, than playing a clean-cut gay plumber who still lives with his dad. Crowe has waited a long time to sit in the back of this theater and watch as his soon-to-be-former skinhead fans realize their error in championing him as an icon of their cause. This sort of radical dramatic reversal—brutish skinhead turns shy gay man with heart of gold—will prove characteristic of Crowe's career in the years to come. Though he does not yet know it, he will accept roles ranging from a misogynist hard-boiled detective in *L.A. Confidential* to a brilliant schizophrenic mathematician in *A Beautiful Mind* to a hairy monster in *Flora Plum*; try as anyone might, Russell Crowe will be a difficult man to pigeon-hole. Sitting in the back of this theater, Crowe takes some satisfaction in this early indicator of the varied career to come.

As one hostile youth spits in the aisle and another tries to make a friend gurgle the word "uncle" by bending his neck over the back of his seat, Crowe sighs and the lights go down . . .

As Sharon Stone looks on placidly, wearing sweatpants, of all things, the neo-Nazis prepare to defend their decrepit warehouse home against an army of young Vietnamese men whose friends the skinheads have murdered. Stone has had her eye on the skinhead leader, Hando, for some time now. From the opening scene of this low-budget Australian film (whose name, *Romper Stomper*, verges on

the ridiculous), Stone has been struck by the energy of the actor playing Hando. The film's skinheads are a band of dumb-and-stupid
misfits who would have trouble describing or even really understanding the horrific ideas that motivate their violent rampages. But
Hando, with German military coat and perfect posture, is subtly—
though strikingly—different. The actor is rendering a true leader
misplaced: a loyal, disciplined, even slightly fatherly figure who, we
imagine, might apply the force of his character to some other cause.
The contrast between Hando's powerful gaze and the wasteland, both
moral and material, in which he lives is one of the most intriguing
aspects of the film.

At this moment Hando's separation from the group is the most
pronounced it has yet been. Stone leans forward. While the rest of
the gang whimpers and longs to run from the revenge-hungry mob
pounding at the gate, Hando stands utterly still. He stares at the
heaving door with his back to his gang, compelled by the force of
his misguided convictions to face this clash. As she beholds this
shot, Stone knows she will soon be calling the actor playing Hando;
this very energy is what she has been seeking for the character of
Cort in her upcoming genre-bending film, *The Quick and the Dead*.
The film, she understands, will be a difficult one to sell: she knows
it works on its own quirky terms, but people are going to require
some convincing. And this man, this . . . Russell Crowe, it says in
the credits, can help with that convincing.

Though she is intrigued even today, Stone does not know that
years from now, she will be calling Russell Crowe "The sexiest man

AS HANDO IN *ROMPER STOMPER*

NEWSPIX

working in Hollywood" and grinning as he accepts a gleaming Academy Award. Something else Stone does not know is that right about now, (future *Insider* producer) Michael Mann is also viewing *Romper Stomper* for the first time; like Stone, Mann is wondering how and when this powerful actor might figure in one of his own films. Mann waits for the credits and marks the name: Russell Crowe. He does not worry that he will forget it.

The crowd is huge: much bigger than expected. Some of the people in line are surprisingly well dressed; they look like they're able to take pretty good care of themselves. Why are they here? The presence of some of the others in line is surprising not because they look fine, but because they look so awful; there's a man by the door shouting at no one in particular and pulling out tufts of his own hair; mentally, he is far away from this room where everyone else is lined up. How did that guy even know to come here? Still, others meet the volunteers' expectations perfectly: they look so downtrodden, patient, and politely grateful that they would make a great photo for a fundraising brochure.

It's Christmas 1993, and this is the breakfast lineup at the Los Angeles Salvation Army. People have been in line for almost an hour to partake of the morning meal here, and the long, patient queue is what Russell Crowe and Sharon Stone find when they arrive in casual clothes and sunglasses to help serve grub.

Crowe and Stone have only recently finished filming *The Quick and the Dead.* They became fast friends: Crowe appreciated that Stone repeatedly went to bat for him with the studio people, not only getting him hired, but also arguing on his behalf about changes to the script. (She was unsuccessful on this latter score; Crowe arrived on the set to find a huge portion of his lines cut.) In return, Crowe worked like mad, exceeding even Stone's expectations, and showed immense respect for the entire project, which was a pet of Stone's.

Although they both believed in and worked hard on the picture—a clever, quirky Western with Biblical overtones (a man has never peeled an apple quite as the devilish Gene Hackman does *The Quick and the Dead*)—both Stone and Crowe came away nursing disappointment. Stone, because the film had opened to a lukewarm reception, both critically and at the box office; Crowe, because his long filming stint in L.A. had led to the amicable but painful end of his five-year relationship with Danielle Spencer. The distance, they had both come to realize, was too hard. This particular trip wasn't the problem, really, but this trip was just the latest in a long string of absences. Both Crowe and Spencer were forced to accept that professional progress for either of them would mean painful separations for both of them. It was a nasty double bind and they both knew it. So that's it: the quick, the dead, the loved, and the lost have brought Crowe to this Christmas morning far from home.

Although Crowe was remarkably focused throughout the filming, Stone knew that he was going through a difficult period off the set. She also learned, during the making of the movie, how hard Crowe found it to be away from home. (Even putting romantic relationships aside, Crowe will say in an interview years from now with Nui Te Koha of *Weekend Magazine*, "It's rough being away from your dog for six months. That's some rough stuff, man.") She had worried that he might find himself alone on Christmas morning, and so had given him a call, telling him that she would be volunteering here and asking him whether he would like to join her. Secretly, she was surprised to hear him agree.

And so Russell Crowe and Sharon Stone, nursing their respective wounds even as they recall that their good fortune grotesquely exceeds that of the people who are now beginning to file past them for plates of hot food, do up their aprons and silently hope that the press won't turn this simple effort into too much of a three-ring circus.

It is very early in the morning. Way too early for Salma Hayek, who is just now approaching the site of today's shoot. They wrapped up late (again) yesterday, and Hayek is exhausted. Filming *Breaking Up* has been one of the most draining experiences of her career to date, and they're not even close to finished with the thing. It seems there are fewer amenities and longer hours at each new location, and there's no end in sight.

She knows it's not only *her* nerves that are frayed. Russell, "Bubo," has been more and more irritable lately—but always very kind to her. She is more amazed at his focus and professionalism every day; as she gets more exhausted, he just seems to get more dogged. He's had some blow-ups, but even those have been over (it's such a cliché, she thinks, but this time it really applies) artistic differences. Russell wants input, and if no one's listening—well, let's just say Russell has the ability to, at times, make *not* hearing him damn near impossible. As she rounds the corner on her way to the place where she was told she'd find her dressing room, Hayek chuckles to herself over Russell's blustery episodes (episodes in whose power and suddenness she, never the target, delights as if they were natural disasters seen from a safe but thrilling distance).

As she turns the bend, she stops dead. What the hell kind of project *is* this? She will not cry. She has not had a full night's sleep in well over two weeks, and she is about to start another day that will no doubt run overtime and accomplish less than it is supposed to, and this whole routine stretches into the future for about as long as she can force herself to imagine, but she will not cry. She will not cry, though she is at this moment staring at her "dressing room" which she now understands is a *blanket* on the *floor*. After the initial onset of rage and discouragement, she brightens: it has just occurred to her that Russell is, at this moment, probably dangling some studio employee over a balcony by his ankles and asking him to state the definition of the word "room." As this image comes into focus (Hayek can practically hear the guy's change falling out of his pockets), she becomes almost giddy; part of her giddiness can be attributed to her fatigue, another part to the pleasure she takes in watching Russell's bold assertions of control on the set. *Alpha male*, she thinks with approval, as she trots off to find him.

Find him she does before long, drinking strong black tea out of a chipped mug, and looking over a sheet of paper describing the day's events. He's sitting on a folding chair at a folding table, and only when she sits down in the seat opposite does he notice her.

"Hey, Buba," he mutters, making an effort to speak gently to her, but clearly not pleased with the morning so far.

"Hey, Bubo," she returns. "About the dressing rooms . . ." She sees a vein in his forehead throb. "Uh, did you throw a fit already?" He looks up at her for the first time now and even before he speaks, she knows that her question was unnecessary.

"Yeah."

"Thanks, Bubo." The irritation she felt earlier in her own gut has disappeared totally. If Russell has gotten angry, it's done. She stares across the table at him as he gulps down his almost-boiling tea. Hmm. Didn't think they made 'em like *this* anymore.

Curtis Hanson is in the editing room going through tape of *L.A. Confidential.* The shoot has gone well, but this cutting and pasting is always a delicate part of the process. People don't realize the impor—

"God," Hanson whispers. "My God." The editors turn to see whether he has somehow severed his finger or had a vision of the Blessed Virgin.

Hardly. Hanson is staring in amazement at Russell Crowe. Or at least at a screen that bears the image of Russell Crowe's face.

RUSSELL PALS AROUND WITH HIS *L.A. CONFIDENTIAL* CO-STAR GUY PEARCE

LISA ROSE / GLOBE PHOTOS

Russell Crowe as Bud White. Russell Crowe as Bud White beholding—and trying desperately to keep himself from violently breaking up—an eruption of domestic abuse. This image of Crowe's face will ultimately become the very first shot of the acclaimed film—and it will be seared into the minds of many more film lovers than the few assembled in this editing room.

Months from this moment in front of the monitor, during an interview with Andy Lowe of *Total Film*, Hanson will link this single shot to his general feelings about Russell Crowe's performance in the role of Bud White: "With Russell, I was confronted with an actor of such intensity and emotion that it seemed an unbeatable combination. I would not have begun the film that way if I didn't think the audience would look at this face—a face most had never seen before—and ask: 'Who is this guy?' and 'What is he looking at?'"

Hanson's prediction of the audience's reaction to Crowe's prolonged gaze was accurate. Crowe is staring straight into the camera with a look that—what's it doing? What does that look *mean*?

One thing about it is clear: Crowe-cum-White could boil over at any second. But behind the obvious volatility of the gaze, a lot is going on; behind the eyes is a roiling bar fight of ambivalence and ambiguity. It's difficult to watch. It's horrifying. It's sublime. It's Russell Crowe at his absolute Russell Crowiest.

"Look at him," Hanson cries. "I mean, *look* at this guy." The editors look.

Crowe looks back.

Will this bruise ever heal? It was purple last week, then it was looking a bit better on the weekend, having progressed into the yellow-green area of the spectrum. But now it's—God, it's almost gray. It seems like it's getting darker. Could it be getting worse? That would only make sense if he'd fallen on it again, which he's pretty sure he . . . all right, so the truth is he doesn't know where or how he's fallen in the past few days. He knows *that* he's fallen— fallen and recovered and fallen again more times than he cares to count (and, of course, cursed like a sailor both on the way up and on the way down). But the details are foggy. In his memory, each day on the ice blends into the next. Worst of all, Crowe doesn't know whether the work he puts in on any of these days is making the slightest bit of difference. He meditates on the possibility that his efforts may actually be futile as he steps out of the shower and further inspects the massive bruise on his hip now that he's in better light.

For the record, though his progress is dearly bought and very slow (and though at the moment he doubts the very existence of this progress), Russell Crowe is indeed learning to skate. Of course, he knew as soon as he took on the role of John Biebe in *Mystery, Alaska* that he would have to acquire the ridiculous skill of sliding around on knives atop a huge oval sheet of ice. And though the hockey requirement worried him somewhat (he was pretty sure it was non-negotiable, given that this was to be a hockey movie), he knew he wanted the quirky part of the straight-man sheriff in the tiny northern town of Mystery.

He'd admitted to himself early on that the hockey was not likely to come naturally. Growing up, he'd been a cricket kid, an Australian football kid, a fencing kid. He had never been—forget never *been*, he had never *heard of* a hockey kid when he was growing up. He didn't know there was such a thing. But nonetheless, when he thought about hockey (and skating as ice hockey's obvious prerequisite) as one of the demands of Biebe's character, Crowe figured he could get the hang of it.

After all, what could hockey possibly want that Russell Crowe couldn't give? Balance? Every sport, when you get good enough at it, is about balance. It's about knowing exactly where your body is, where it's inclined to go (because of inertia, fear, fatigue, whatever), and whether you (the upstairs part of you that calls the shots) need to intervene in its proposed trajectory. Crowe was an athlete; he knew he had balance. Rhythm? Oh, Crowe had rhythm. I mean, have you *seen* this man dance? Leg strength? Please. Don't insult him with the question.

Yes, Russell Crowe felt certain when he signed up for this gig, he *could* learn to skate.

But that was months ago. Today, this bruise on his hip (and, ladies and gentlemen, this is not the only one), suggests otherwise. This massive internal wound is asking loudly and repeatedly, *"Are you sure?"*

"Of course I'm sure," Crowe grumbles. "Don't you remember *The Quick and the Dead*?"

"Before my time," says the bruise.

"Yeah, well, remember all that gunslinging and gunfighting and fucking Old West virtuosity?" Crowe asks, ignoring the bruise's last statement.

"No."

"No stand-ins, mate. I did all that stuff. Who the fuck knows how to be a gunslinger these days? *I do*. Whenever I had a break, I'd get that gun and whip it around, spin it, flip it, throw it—"

"Drop it."

"Of course, you little piece of piss. Of course I'd drop it. But when it came time to do that scene in the gun shop where Cort's got to show that he's—well, point is, mate, I had the thing completely under my control. I was calling the shots. Fuck gravity, you know?"

"Mmm."

"And do you remember when I went to Wales to—"

"No."

"I went to Wales years ago. I needed a Welsh accent, right? Paid my own way so I could live there and get it bang on and do the bloody part. And it was perfect. Do you know what I'm saying right now? It was perfect. Bottom line, mate, I get ready for the film. There is not a time when I'm not ready for the film. Whatever I have to do. Physical, mental, vocal, whatever. If I can be a goddamn Australian gunslinger in 1993, then I can skate around a bloody rink once or twice."

"Mmm."

In the end, the bruise won the argument. Crowe did learn to skate but not well enough to meet his own standards. "The major point of *Mystery, Alaska* for me," he told Francesca Dinglasan, "was the physical challenge of learning how to skate from zero, from scratch. Starting in November, shooting in January, learning how to ice skate. And I failed dismally."

The fifty-something man in a white lab coat and bifocals, who
is at present looking down at an open file folder on his desk with a deep frown and a slight shaking of his head, has been the Crowe family doctor for some years. He doesn't know this older son, the actor, very well, but he has seen him often enough to know that this soft 238-pound frame is not the one he usually inhabits. "For a role," the young man says. "Physical preparation," he says. Physical preparation for a massive coronary, the doctor had muttered to himself internally. The body, the physician coins an aphorism, is not a prop.

On the other side of the desk, Russell Crowe makes a mental note: buy new (larger) jeans. He shifts in his chair to adjust the pants that are digging into his fleshy sides and hears a slight crackle of paper in his jacket pocket: the cheeseburger wrapper he has forgotten to deposit in a trash can. Crowe watches the expression on the doctor's face as he peers at the pink file, and Crowe is slightly annoyed. It's not as though I've really let myself go, he thinks. This is a deliberate effort at controlled weight gain for a specific purpose.

The part of Jeffrey Wigand demands this flesh. Crowe has to convey a vulnerability, a flaccid middle-agedness that says, "Who am I—just one unexceptional man, just a single helpless soul—who am I to take on the great corporate demons of the Western world?" Crowe's usual physique is more compatible with a message along the lines of, "Oh yeah, Western world? Why don't you come over *here* and say that."

Besides, Crowe has no doubt that the weight will come off easily. The main change he has made in his lifestyle—in addition to the consumption of massive quantities of greasy food and bourbon, of course—has been the total cessation of all physical activity. No work on the farm, no football, no cricket—nothing. Once he resumes a lifestyle even resembling his normal, intensely physical one, his body will resume its former are-you-talking-to-me dimensions. Six weeks on, six weeks off.

The actor is sick of this appointment. "Listen, mate, the pounds are nothing to worry about. Once the movie is over and I get off my fat arse some, they'll go. In the meantime, I'll tread carefully among the flowers." Crowe snorts a little at his own joke.

The doctor looks up. "I wish it were only your, uh, fat arse we had to concern ourselves with, Russell. In fact, you have the cholesterol of a man thirty-five years your senior with an extremely dubious lifestyle. In short, you are in danger of having a major heart attack, among other things."

Crowe wipes the smirk off his face for a minute. He is silent and then, quietly: "Jesus, mate. Hasn't anyone told my arteries it's just a bloody job?" It hadn't occurred to him until now that his preparation for *The Insider* might have consequences for his body other than aesthetic ones. Of course, the frustration of not lifting a finger on the farm or playing in any reindeer games with his brother and friends has been a bit grating, but a heart attack?

When Crowe arrives home forty minutes later, Terry has just gone inside for lunch. They greet each other, and Terry notices a brown pellet of some kind fall from Russell's sleeve as Russell turns to close the front door. "What's that, Russ?" Terry asks, pointing to the pellet on the floor.

"Nothing," Russell replies, crossing the kitchen floor to deposit an empty box of Grape Nuts in the garbage.

Russell Crowe is sitting in a tall chair that swivels. And, like a couple of hundred pounds of the choicest cheese in Hollywood, he is being very carefully and very deliberately aged. This pre-shoot ritual is, after all these weeks, familiar to everyone involved.

The procedure goes like this: at an ungodly hour in the morning, one of the most robust and imposing men in Hollywood (let's face it, probably one of the most robust and imposing men in the hemisphere) strides into this room and sits down in this chair. In the mirror, he glimpses his own clean-shaven, thirty-five-year-old face, which is at the moment a little pudgier than he's used to. According to moods or tides or celestial conditions no one else can quite figure out or predict, when Crowe sits down each day, he smiles or glowers or jokes or remains stonefaced. In this chair, he can be as patient as an anesthetized monk, or as restless and indignant as an expert sled-dog on a slim pink leash.

The makeup artists hover around their specimen, who is docile today. They brush, pencil, mold, and shade, trying to make Crowe look like the opposite of what he is: a prodigiously tough Australian outdoorsman. (Sometimes they find themselves longing for an easier task, like fashioning a Klingon forehead or trying to keep the Golden Girls young.) They have learned by now that somehow, remarkably, the actor who inhabits this powerful frame manages to get out of this chair and make himself move and speak and stare like a frightened, exhausted scientist almost twenty years his senior. So. All *they* have to do is make sure Crowe's own face doesn't give him away. (Is it too late to become an accountant?) They begin by setting aside at least two full hours every morning before the shoot, and sitting the ÜberAussie down in this tall chair that swivels. And that is where he's seated when *Insider* producer, director, and co-writer Michael Mann comes in to talk.

Mann and Crowe greet each other affably. They trade a few notes on how yesterday went, and how they'd like today to go. (This producer has already learned that almost nothing happens on the set about which Crowe does not have an opinion.) Mann shakes his head slightly as, in the course of their conversation, the image of Russell Crowe in the mirror recedes and the image of Jeffrey Wigand appears. The transformation is familiar, but that doesn't make it less

Russell Crowe

WITH *THE INSIDER* DIRECTOR MICHAEL MANN

FRED PROUSER / REUTERS / GETTY IMAGES

strange to see Crowe, a virtual caricature of manliness, so softened and diminished each day.

After a light gloss of the day's planned events, the two move on to other subjects. Mann wonders aloud whether the actor has another project lined up after this one, or whether he's just planning to stick with the chubby fifty-year-old persona for a while. Crowe laughs. Mann knows that the writing is crucial for Crowe, and both men lament the rarity of scripts as good as the one they're working on now. As a makeup artist adjusts the thin grey wig on Crowe's shaven head, the actor mentions a few "pieces of piss" that he's been contacted about recently; Mann nods and rolls his eyes sympathetically. But as Crowe goes on, something catches Mann's attention.

"This Roman thing you're going to reject—did you say who's directing that?"

"The toga party?" Crowe snorts. "Oh, yeah. These blokes call me up, they say 'It's 185 A.D.; it's Ridley Scott; at the beginning of the film you're a Roman general.' No bloody script, I don't—"

Mann looks at Crowe in the mirror. "You're saying 'No'?"

A shrug from Crowe. "I just can't get my head 'round it right now. And you know I make my decisions based on the text. I don't want to end up in some piece of piss wearing a loin cloth and beating my bloody chest."

Mann nods again. He has witnessed the actor's single-minded preparation for this role. The hours spent viewing and reviewing tapes of Wigand's testimony. The almost eerie focus. Even the necessary forty-pound weight gain, which many actors would have seen as merely an opportunity for gustatory and alcoholic indulgence, Crowe approached with a fierce discipline that told Mann he was indeed working with the serious actor he had suspected he was witnessing in *Romper Stomper* and *L.A. Confidential.*

On the set, Crowe has been ornery at times, chastising others for breaches of professionalism, angrily scolding colleagues for failing to show what he believes to be the necessary level of intensity. But however one sees Crowe—as a bully, a perfectionist, a consummate pro, a total jerk—a hypocrite he is not. Seldom has Mann seen such complete and unwavering presence either in a particular role or on the set at large. No wonder Crowe can't get his mind out of this project and see himself in what he imagines will be Ridley Scott's big-budget "toga party."

Crowe's makeup is finished. He dons his emphatically unstylish stainless steel frames and the disquieting metamorphosis is complete. He swivels in his chair to find a suddenly serious Michael Mann taking a seat.

"I know you choose your projects carefully."

Crowe nods, not put off by Mann's suddenly frank tone.

"And you don't strike me as someone who's a big fan of other people's advice."

Crowe endures this gentle jibe with all the good humor of Margaret Thatcher in ill-fitting hose. Mann clears his throat and continues. "And I appreciate your focus on this project because—hell, of course I do. It's my movie."

Crowe nods.

"But if I were you right now, I would not give up an opportunity to work with Ridley Scott."

"Listen, mate, I'm not interested in the flashy—"

"I'm not talking about gloss or whatever you—money, even—whatever you think I might be talking about. I'm telling you that in my opinion Scott is among the roughly two percent of directors—I mean in cinema history—who are actually masters of this art. He's serious the way you are. I don't have to tell you that's rare. And if you don't take another look at your invitation to the toga party, Russell, you're making a mistake."

A long pause follows. Mann looks at his watch, throws Crowe a parting nod that doesn't dare condescend by signifying "Think about it," and leaves the doughy scientist alone in his high swivel chair. Crowe turns back to face the mirror and looks long at the aging stranger there.

Crowe trusts and respects Mann. He can't say that about many people he's worked with in the movie business. The first moment Crowe had known that Mann was someone whose approach to filmmaking he could appreciate happened when the two men first met to discuss the script for *The Insider*. Crowe had already decided he wasn't right for the part of Jeffrey Wigand, but he wanted to tell Mann that he liked the script and that he hoped Mann would keep him in mind for other roles in the future. He was then, as he is now, having trouble seeing himself in his next role. He had just come out of *L.A. Confidential*, playing Bud White, the most hardboiled of hardboiled detectives, and beleaguered family man Jeffrey Wigand seemed a long way away. He wondered, even, whether Mann wasn't mistaking him for someone else when he asked Crowe to play the part.

But when the two men met to talk about *The Insider*, Crowe found that Mann had known exactly what he was doing when he had called Crowe. Mann explained that he had seen Crowe not only in *L.A. Confidential* and *The Quick and the Dead*, but also in *Romper Stomper*. In fact, it was Crowe's portrayal of Hando—and not Bud White—that had first caused Mann to notice the Australian. When Crowe protested that Wigand would be a huge, almost impossible, physical stretch for him, not only because of his weight and general bearing, but also because of his age, Mann did something that Crowe has remembered ever since.

"Russell, I'm not asking you to do this because of your age or your body fat percentage. This role is a crucial one in a film whose quality I think is very important. I'm asking you to do the role because of what you have in here." And Mann actually laid his hand on Crowe's chest. Crowe was taken aback for a minute, but then he was impressed: this was not Hollywood talk. This guy was going to make a serious movie, and he wanted Crowe to be at its center. The two men talked some more that day, but Crowe had already decided that he would take the part.

Now, over a year later, here he is again being coached by Mann toward the next role. He shakes his head in the mirror. He's all for great directors, and if Ridley Scott is one of them, then it's something to consider. But a gladiator movie? He tries to conjure an image of

Ridley Scott in his mind's eye—just so he can get rid of the clutter of sandals, greased torsos, and farcically noble chins that keeps crowding his brain when he thinks of the word Gladiator.

Meanwhile, back at the ranch . . . Crowe is relaxing after dinner, seated in the caravan in which he is living temporarily while the old farmhouse a few hundred yards away is being renovated. He looks forward to moving into the house, but he's at ease in the caravan; he has a kettle, some food, a bed—he's outside most of the time anyway and, besides, he doesn't require frills. When he's at work, he snorts as he watches the soft Hollywood lifers who can't so much as tolerate a brand of mineral water that has ceased to be fashionable. ("Marly? What is this? I wanted the *glacier* one. Can someone tell Marly it's the *glacier* one? In the blue bottle? Tha-anks.") Crowe hasn't spent many nights on the ranch this year because he's been away filming so much, but thankfully he's here tonight. He's drinking black tea and leafing through a script that looks like a loser when the phone rings.

"Hello."

"Is this, uh . . . Russell Crowe?" A pause.

"How did you get this number?"

"Is this Russell Crowe?"

Crowe's tone is deadly: "This is one bloke you don't want to bother when he's having a cup of tea after dinner, mate. How did you get this number?"

"No need to be rude there, Russ." The voice is shaky, but full of false bravado. Crowe hangs up. The phone rings again. He picks it up immediately.

"Listen, mate, you'd be better off calling Hanks or somebody, 'cause if you keep this up I can guarantee I will—"

"Do you remember that night in the pub in Coff's Harbour?" The voice is frightened by Crowe's easy and immediate hostility, but it is determined. It's male, deep, youngish.

"Who the fuck is this?" Crowe is irritated (and, truth be told, curious) but totally unrattled.

"Just someone with some information you might be interested in."

"I can live without the detective novel dialogue, mate. You want to tell me something, you want an autograph, you want to blackmail me—what?" Crowe is secretly beginning to enjoy himself a little. When he thought this guy was just an intrusive fan, that was annoying; but some little piss trying his hardest to sound threatening, now *that's* fun. "You still there, mate? Figured out what you want yet?"

The caller clears his throat, taking another stab at making his voice crawl with menace. "I am in possession of a certain video documentation of a certain event which I am aware transpired . . ." Crowe has caught a glimpse of himself reflected in the window; he squints playfully at his own mirror image, as if sharing a joke about the anonymous caller with an admiring friend.

"Listen, mate, you can't threaten me if you can't make better sense than this."

**STILL FROM SECURITY CAMERA OUTSIDE THE SALOON BAR
AT COFF'S HARBOUR**

NEWSPIX

The caller begins to fume in that special way only lifelong losers can as Crowe's flippancy increases. This call is not unfolding anywhere near as gracefully as the caller had planned. After he found the video at the bar and hatched the plan, he had rehearsed his lines for days (inserting on his own Crowe's frightened, pleading responses), but Crowe, it seems, is a scene-stealer.

"Maybe you should stop laughing," the voice resumes. "I have the security tape of you biting that guy's neck that night in Coff's Harbour." Silence. Silence.

"Oh! Well, dear *me*. How much would you like? A million? A billion? Perhaps a zillion would do it?" Crowe's tone has changed from one of false gravity to—well, his tone is hard to decipher now that he's wheezing with laughter. "Whate*v*uh could keep you from ruinin' mah reputation, you miserable man?" Crowe has begun to affect the voice and accent of a southern debutante.

The caller makes one more effort: "I'm not afraid to release this tape to the media, you know." Crowe's laughter stops on a dime.

"Do I sound like *I'm* afraid of that, mate? I don't know how you got this number, but you clearly didn't know who you were calling. At least be the first to hang up and save yourself a bit of pride." Crowe hears nothing. He snorts and roughly replaces the receiver on the cradle. After reflecting for a brief moment on the uselessness of much of his species, he returns crankily to his lame script.

"Hello?"

"Hello, uh, Mr. Crowe? This is Carl McSweeney . . . I'm part of the team that's designing your Web site, russellcrowe.com? And I, uh, heard that your assistant Mr. Bob Long had called and wanted to speak to me?"

"Oh—yeah. Listen, mate, I got some photos for the site. And I wrote some commentary to go with them."

"Really? I mean, that's great, actually. The site, actually, isn't really up yet, though, is the only thing. Right now we're working on the—"

"Yeah, I know it's not up. This is just some stuff to tide people over, right? Some photos and that."

"Mr. Crowe, it's really good of you to do this and everything, but . . . well I mean you don't have to. We've been . . . uh . . . we've been working with the photo agencies and we have stills of your films and all, so for you to provide personal photos is really actually unnecess—"

"Listen, Carl, I can guarantee you don't already have these ones. This is real insider stuff. You can put 'em up right away, right? Like, before the site is done?"

"Sure. Of course, Mr. Crowe. It's your site."

"Great then. I'll send them tomorrow."

Two days later, a manila envelope finds its way onto Carl McSweeney's desk. It contains a set of photos, enfolded in a sheet of plain white paper. On the outside of the paper, in black marker, the following words have been scrawled: TO BE SCANNED. FOR WEB SITE.

In a smaller, business-sized envelope, there is an 8 $^1/_2$ × 11 sheet of paper with some writing on it in the same hand.

At first it is difficult to make out what the pictures depict; they're dark and they lack definition. They're of something very . . . close up. Carl McSweeney turns one around, trying to find which direction is up, which orientation makes the most sense. He clears some clutter off his desk—a zip disk, a Wolverine action figure, a koosh ball, a Men at Work CD—and lays the photos out. Perplexed, McSweeney reaches for the accompanying page of text. He unfolds the sheet and his eyes widen.

Russell Crowe has sent photos of his own shoulder surgery to be included on the website. The text that goes with the photos is full of bravado, making cracks about the staff at the hospital and the procedure itself. Apparently, he refused to wear the prescribed clothes during the surgery—namely, paper pants—because they didn't have anything to do with his shoulder.

McSweeney chuckles; he sees Crowe's angle. The photos seem to say, "They want Russell Crowe inside and out? Let's give 'em all of Russell Crowe." McSweeney scans the photos and puts them up on the site. He creates the link and thinks for a moment about what it should be called. After a short pause, the young geek nods slightly and grins to himself. He types: THE INSIDE STORY.

The problem with playing a Roman general from the second century A.D. who—in addition to being thousands of years removed from your own historical moment—just happens to be the strong *silent* type, is that it can be a bit difficult to get inside the guy's head. Of course, when Russell Crowe was first introduced to the character of Maximus, the general was even more silent than usual because he did not belong to any full or stable screenplay. He was only an idea: massive and powerful in his way, but also thin as air. On this particular evening, we find Russell Crowe determined to do his usual amount of rigorous research but slightly at a loss as to how to research a character who has not yet been written into existence. He is reclining on his brother Terry's living room sofa, slightly stiff from the day's efforts to rid himself of his *Insider* flab, leafing through a dog-eared book. He's already gone through some relevant material about antiquity—gladiatorial games, scheming senators, massive meals taken lying down—but it's all been either glossy and superficial or hopelessly academic. Where are the *characters*?

Crowe has just picked up the book in his hands from the stack on the coffee table. From where Terry sits watching television, he can just make out the words on the worn spine: Marcus Aurelius, *Meditations*. Terry doesn't know whether this is a book from Russell's past (history was the only subject in high school at which the adolescent Russell Crowe really excelled) or something new. He just knows he's glad that at the moment he is not reading anything by anyone whose names, both first and last, end in "us."

Russell reads intently, mental miles away from the spectacularly theatrical wrestling match playing itself out on the television. After about ten minutes, he mutters, "This is it." He nods slowly and then speaks again: "Eureka, mate." If one were to look over Russell Crowe's shoulder at this moment, which his brother Terry has neither the nerve nor the desire to do, one would find the following passage on the page before him:

> . . . the offences which are committed through desire are more blameable than those which are committed through anger. For he who is excited by anger seems to turn away from reason with a certain pain and unconscious contraction; but he who offends through desire, being overpowered by pleasure, seems to be in a manner more intemperate and more womanish in his offences.

Crowe is beginning to feel the hard outline of Maximus taking shape amid the meditations of this philosopher-king. As he reads on, he finds not only an increasingly clear sense of Maximus, but strange reflections of himself:

> . . . and besides bear in mind that every man lives only this present time, which is an indivisible point, and that all the rest of his life is either past or it is uncertain. Short then is the time which every man lives, and small the nook of the earth where he lives; and short too the longest posthumous fame, and even this only continued by a succession of poor human beings, who will very soon die, and who know not even themselves, much less him who died long ago.

And finally, Crowe finds the passage that seems to define everything Maximus must be and do:

> If thou workest at that which is before thee, following right reason seriously, vigorously, calmly, without allowing anything else to distract thee, but keeping thy divine part pure, as if thou shouldst be bound to give it back immediately; if thou holdest to this, expecting nothing, fearing nothing, but satisfied with thy present activity according to nature, and with heroic truth in every word and sound which thou utterest, thou wilt live happy. And there is no man who is able to prevent this.

Crowe, amazed and inspired, utters these last words aloud: *"And there is no man who is able to prevent this."* Terry looks up from the television and, truth be told, is unnerved by the intensity of his brother's focus. He stares at Russell for one, then two full minutes. In a silent joke for no audience but himself, he points the remote control at his brother and presses buttons at random, trying to change some settings, jostle him in any way, even make him scratch his ear. Anything to break this eerie concentration. Click. Click. Russell doesn't notice.

Reflecting on the day's oppressive heat and his own desperate

fatigue, Russell Crowe gives silent thanks for this long-awaited day off. For weeks he has endured the most challenging—and punishing—work of his life. Dawn-till-drop days under the searing Maltese sun, fighting with armor and swords that some grown men couldn't even lift. Sparring with men, wrestling with tigers, scene after scene, the whole time maintaining the trademark dramatic intensity that is the point of all this—an intensity that would, on its own, be exhausting even if Crowe were playing, say, a cardboard tree in a third-grade production of *The Three Bears*.

Crowe was, as ever, impeccably prepared for this shoot. He spent half a year working off his *Insider* flab ("Six weeks on, six months off," he would later say of the almost forty pounds of burgers and bourbon that were part of his metamorphosis into Jeffrey Wigand), laboring furiously on his ranch and training with an expert swordmaster. (Crowe had fenced when he was younger, but decided he could use practice when it came to the giant broadswords of the world of his character, Maximus.) In addition to all the physical work, Crowe trained psychologically to be a general-like leader, shepherding a gang of friends through a long and difficult motorcycle tour of the Australian outback. But even Crowe's famous discipline could not prepare him for the demands of this role.

The process has been not only gruelling but dangerous. At various points during the shoot Crowe has broken a bone in his foot, cracked a hipbone, and (at different times) wrenched both bicep tendons out of their sockets. (Needless to say, Crowe popped both back into place on his own, using only that manliest of anaesthetic aids, a shot of Jack Daniels.)

This catalog of trials and injuries might make less gladiatorial souls cringe and cower, but as far as Crowe is concerned, things could have been worse. Remember those tigers in the arena with Maximus/Crowe and the boys? Two words: not digital. Though the beasts were chained and the fight scenes carefully choreographed, when it comes to wrestling tigers, it is impossible to, shall we say, control all the variables. In one (of a handful of) tigerly mishaps on the set, a giant cat leapt onto Crowe's colleague Sven Ole Thorsen, pinning the terrified actor to the dirt. Luckily for Thorsen, Crowe was also acting in the scene. Seeing Thorsen's predicament (which really seems too calm a word to describe such a blubberingly frightful position), Crowe scooted over to the cat and swatted it on the behind, causing it to climb off and saunter away from Thorsen, irritated and distracted, to be brought under control by the trainers.

It is with these assorted trials and terrors in mind that we find Crowe on the morning of his well-deserved day off. Taking a short walk along a dusty road not far from the immense replica of the Roman Coliseum (price tag: $1 million plus), thinking from time to time about how to organize the teams in the soccer match he has planned for the afternoon, our hero is apprehended by a young studio employee.

"Mr. Crowe," the boy calls, approaching the bronzed and imposing actor. These days Crowe's body is big and powerful; he knew he needed to be extremely fit to play Maximus, but didn't want to look like another Hollywood pretty boy. He decided not to go to the gym and isolate unheard of muscle groups, but rather to work like hell at all kinds of physical labor. He would later tell interviewers that his thinking went like this: if he could get himself into shape so that he could do everything Maximus could do, he would probably end up looking the way Maximus should look. The boy catches up to Crowe, saying, "I have a memo for you from the studio, sir?"

Crowe, easy and amiable, takes the envelope. "Thanks, mate." The boy begins to walk away. Crowe reads. After half a minute, he looks up and shouts, "Hey, mate, come back a minute." The young man jogs back to Crowe. "You know what this says?" Crowe asks him.

"No, sir."

"They're asking me not to play bloody football today . . . in case I get *injured*." Crowe's tone is one of disbelief. The young man doesn't understand, but shakes his head and smiles (he hopes) sympathetically. Crowe pays no attention to the carefully crafted look. "You got a pen?" The boy nods vigorously and reaches into his pocket. He produces a pen and a pencil and offers Crowe his choice. Crowe grabs one without looking. "Bend over, right?"

The boy, confused only for an instant, turns and bends at the waist. He feels the memo come down on his back and then Crowe's pen scribbling. Crowe speaks as he writes, letting the boy become part of this tiny mutiny. The gesture is big-brotherly.

Dear—Studio.

I—can—wrestle—with—four—tigers [here Crowe chuckles at his own scheme and at the idiocy of his negligent baby-sitters]—but—I—can't—play—a—game—of—soccer? [Here a short pause as Crowe considers his next line.] Get—over—it.

Love,

Russell

The boy grins and straightens up as Crowe folds the note. "Run that back to 'em, will you, mate?" The boy nods and races back to the set, giddy with conspiracy.

The day is extremely hot. Ridley Scott is sitting in an air-conditioned trailer just outside of "Rome"—the Rome that has been created on a miniature scale in Malta for the filming of *Gladiator*. Scott is going over the day's scene list, imagining the luscious shots he will meticulously engineer. How to make the tigers seem as though they're swatting at the gladiators' very tunics? How to make the crowd take on an almost bestial quality? How to make the coliseum seem like a carnivorous plant that lives on the blood squeezed out at its center? And this question, always: How to get the whole battle in the frame, but also manage to get enough of Crowe's intent, incredible face?

The face in question appears through the trailer door, just now nudged open by a few polite (but—both men know—irrelevant) knocks, and interrupts Scott's "visioning." Scott sets down the papers he has been absently sifting through (the quick sketches he makes to illustrate his ideas for others on the set are affectionately dubbed "Ridleygrams" by his colleagues) and motions to Crowe to come in. The man is spectacular; just under six feet, and about a hundred and eighty pounds of some substance that appears extremely dense. The tan that's been slathered over Crowe not only by the makeup artists, but by the real, honest-to-goodness Maltese sun, makes him look like a comic book hero—but this here's no greased-up *image* of a hero. Crowe is about as genuine an article as Scott has encountered. Scott was convinced of this fact long ago, but last week's tiger-swatting incident proved yet again that the rumors are true. Well, not all the rumors, but at least the one that says that Russell Crowe is a specimen whose manliness exceeds the power of most of Hollywood's replicas to even imagine it. They, with their suvs and their personal trainers and their designer water; do they know that this man will *fight with a tiger and smile while he's doing it?* Problems aside, Crowe is a—but problems are not to be put aside this morning, it seems. Because Crowe has one. And Scott has been on this set in the stinking hot sun long enough to know that when Crowe has a problem, Scott has a problem.

The first time the two men locked horns was about six seconds into their initial discussion about Maximus. Crowe thought that since Maximus is from Spain, he should speak with a Spanish accent. "Antonio Banderas with better elocution," Crowe had said to Chris

Nashawaty of *Entertainment Weekly*. Authentic, Scott thought, but a high risk of goofiness. He preferred the classic, vaguely British accent that seems to do nicely for the noble characters Hollywood draws forth from the sands of history. Not totally genuine, he realized, but authenticity hovers around number seven hundred and eighty-two on the priority list when one is making a would-be blockbuster historical epic with $20 million of other people's (namely, Dreamworks's) money. Crowe will later mock this accent in his interview with Nashawaty, calling it "Royal Shakespeare Company two pints after lunch." Scott will not laugh when he hears this.

Crowe has seated himself across from Scott in a folding chair. They greet each other quickly, both aware that there is An Issue hanging in the air between them.

"Ridley, I've been thinking about the script." Scott exhales through his nose. This is not the first discussion the two men have had about the script, and it will not be the last. The script was nonexistent when the film was first conceived; the concept preceded lines and characters and everything else. And even once it was written, it underwent substantial revisions; indeed, those revisions have continued until the present. The whole middle act—in which Maximus is trained in the Middle East—has been added, and countless other changes have kept the script in flux since day one. And now Crowe, surprise surprise, has been thinking . . .

"What about the script?"

"It's too cynical—too close to one of those Willis movies where there's no motivation, no character, no real plot, just this guy who tears around totally fearless, like a maniac, really, and keeps going and going until everyone else is dead."

"Mmm?"

"It's got too damn many jokes as well. These awful one-liners that turn the film into a long, extremely expensive joke with some violence thrown in. 'I'll be back' and all that bullshit. Maximus is a serious, noble person, and more than that he's been wronged and devastated in the worst ways imaginable. For him to be quipping all the way to the coliseum robs him of all his motivation and power. It makes him totally flat—also bloody unsympathetic and maybe a bit crazy."

"Well, Russell—"

"Also, it's too modern. It sounds like L.A. last fucking month, Ridley. I know we're never going to be totally linguistically authentic, but we've got to at least conjure the period a bit, at least create some distance between the audience and the action."

Scott sighs. Crowe, as ever, is deeply, unfailingly, *weirdly* serious. "Russell, I know that the script has been a problem for you—for both of us—since the beginning. And I realize that we've had our disputes about the importance of visual images versus, you know, lines. But text is important to me too, and basically the movie—"

"I want to write a speech."

"Sorry?"

"I want to write a speech for Maximus, to give him some depth that he needs and that he doesn't have right now."

"Russell, I know we've all sort of fiddled with the script together as we've gone along, but that's because it was so rough to begin with. I don't know that we should start—"

"It's necessary. The character needs it. Otherwise he's a sword-wielding cardboard cutout. I'll bring it to you tomorrow."

Crowe rises and hulks out of the trailer. Scott makes a pact with himself: when he sees the final version of this film for the first time, he will remember today. And last Wednesday. And all the other days. Once he has seen the film, and once he has gathered all these memories of Crowe in his mind, then and only then will he decide: *Is this man worth it?*

At 6 a.m. the next morning, along with memos from the studio and other assorted paperwork, Ridley Scott's assistant hands him a sheet of paper half-full of hand-written text. He prevents himself from making any outward noise or movement, but inside he growls in a way that only an English man in Malta at 6 a.m. before a long day of grueling work can. He walks over to his trailer, climbs inside, and sits down with Crowe's speech. There's a note at the top explaining that it's to go in the quiet, intimate scene with Marcus Aurelius at the beginning of the film. Marcus Aurelius must ask Maximus about the home to which he is so anxious to return. According to Russell Crowe, actor, stunt man, strong man, tiger-fighter, and now screenwriter, Maximus's home is

A very simple place: pink stones that warm in the sun, a kitchen garden that smells of herbs in the day, jasmine in the evening. Through the gate is a giant poplar, figs, apples, pears. The soil, Marcus . . . black like—black as my wife's hair. Grapes on the south slope, olives on the north. Wild ponies play near my house. They tease my son; he wants to be one of them.

[How long has he been away?]

Two years, two hundred sixty-four days, and this morning.

Scott sighs and shakes his head. *Shit*. He loves it. Later, he will ask Crowe what gave him the idea. Crowe will answer without turning toward him: "Know how many nights I've spent on my farm this year, mate?"

"Champagne, mate?"

Ridley Scott nods. He anticipates some schoolyard-style mockery from Crowe because of this order, which was immediately preceded by Crowe's extremely manly request for "Jack Daniels, straight up." Scott considered, for a brief moment, ordering something other than champagne, which is what he wanted, just to avoid Crowe's jibes. But that consideration was vetoed almost as quickly as it was hatched: "I am an adult male, and a rather successful one at that," the Pride Sector of Scott's brain had insisted. "And I will order the drink I would like to consume, irrespective of Mr. Crowe's feelings about the implications of my choice for my personal fortitude, sexual orientation, ability to father children, etc."

And so Scott has ordered champagne. Crowe snorted slightly at the order, and it was easy to tell from the look on his face that his smartass remark–production mechanism had begun to sputter to

Russell Crowe gives his Oscar acceptance speech

Ridley Scott directs Russell Crowe in a scene from *Gladiator*

Acting in a scene from *Proof of Life*

Arriving at the premiere of *Mission Impossible 2* with Tom Cruise

With TOFOG guitarist Dean Cochran

Performing with TOFOG

Taking a walk with Meg Ryan

ENJOYING A MANLY BEVERAGE

FIONA HAMILTON / NEWSPIX

life. While working on *Gladiator*, Scott has seen this mechanism of Crowe's turn out jovial, good-natured quips that have set a whole crew full of tired, frustrated people at ease, draining tension from the set as nothing else (and no one else) could. At other times, Scott has seen Crowe devastate less experienced actors, throwing out a barb so laced with acid that victims have been markedly changed for whole days of the shoot.

Scott has never seen an actor assume this kind of power on a set. The big names, sure, have pull. They throw tantrums or finesse directors to get their way; they erect barriers (subtle or not-so-subtle) between themselves and "lesser" members of the cast. Extreme stardom instills a very particular and, in many cases, unpleasant kind of authority in people. But Crowe is not just an overprivileged egomaniac. Not just a vain primadonna. Crowe has somehow become the moody patriarch of this entire production. Crowe giveth and Crowe taketh away. Crowe smileth and Crowe looketh on with unpleased eyes. Crowe approveth of thy work or thou hearest about it, long and loud, from Crowe.

He hosts these events—dinners, football games, evening drinks— for everyone who's working on the film. Very nice of him, really. One dinner was at The Barracuda, one of the best restaurants in Malta. And he invites everyone—not just the central actors and the director, but the crew, the stunt people, everyone. So it's kind—but then, it's also a little strange. The events seem intended to signify Crowe's appreciation of everyone's work. Nice. But then, who appointed Crowe lord over so many entertainment-industry serfs?

Who said from on high, "Russell, look out for these kids: pass judgment when you must, but try to be a benevolent ruler"? Crowe giveth, and Crowe taketh away.

At the moment Crowe giveth Ridley Scott a glass of champagne with surprisingly little resistance or derision. One *"Champagne, mate?"* is an acceptable price to pay for this drink, in Scott's mind. Scott and Crowe have once again met to discuss *Gladiator*'s script, especially Maximus, and Scott suspects he will need a small amount of chemical assistance during their discussion. The script has been such a changeable entity throughout the filming that it seems every scene requires some new decision about lines, and even plot. Those decisions can then necessitate changes in other scenes, scenes which may already have been shot, and now thus require reworking, and on and on: *Gladiator* has spawned a web of creative and logistical complications that Scott chooses not to contemplate at this moment. He is in love with the visual side of this film; the textual side may yet kill him.

The problem of the hour is that the audience still needs more access to Maximus—they need to understand this burly man's head as he faces death after spectacularly gruesome death and just keeps on lopping off heads and arms. Without some more interiority, Maximus is just another Hollywood brute.

So, Scott and Crowe receive their respective drinks and get down to business, imagining how they might best project the inner reaches of Maximus onto the screen. They each pull out a tattered, scribbled-on script and suggest scenes where they think changes could be made to illuminate the general's mental state. Crowe tells Scott (again) about Marcus Aurelius's *Meditations* and how crucial the book has been to his performance of Maximus—how it established in Crowe's mind a set of values by which the character is always guided. Scott tells Crowe about the painting that first sold him on *Gladiator*. He had been reluctant to do the film, but something about the energy of the scene depicted in a painting someone had presented to him (the painting shows a gladiator in an arena standing over a defeated opponent as the crowd encourages him to finish off the wounded foe) convinced him that the movie could surpass the sandal-and-toga epics that had become a bad joke in Hollywood by the late sixties. For Scott, the power of Maximus finds its clearest illustration in the drama of the coliseum. The two men bat ideas back and forth: new lines, new speeches, new shots, new scenes. Some ideas are better than others, but none is really satisfying. It is remarkably difficult to give the audience intimate access to a character who depends so heavily on an external shell composed of words like "duty" and "honor."

Scott thinks out loud: "It would be really great if we could somehow get right inside his head, you know? Maximus will never say, 'I hate them for destroying my home, I miss my family, I want to weep until I die.' He might think it, but he covers it over with what he 'must' do. So I don't think what we're looking for can come through dialogue."

"What are you thinking about?"

"I'm not sure . . . maybe a dream sequence or something?

Something that comes straight from him, not filtered through some situation we cook up."

Crowe is silent. He likes the idea of a dream sequence. They continue to brainstorm in this vein, and finally settle upon the image that is to become a ghost that floats through the film, surfacing only occasionally but always palpably present: in a strange, silver light, Maximus's hand just grazes the tips of the blades of long grass that grow on his farm. When they have refined the idea—and even more, later, when he sees the image on film—Crowe gives Scott a checkmark on his mental dry-erase board. Crowe had doubted that an image could say all that needed to be said about Maximus, but Scott knew. Scott is (Crowe recalls Michael Mann's words) a master.

The three women synchronized their watches for the mission at 7:15 p.m. Since then, they have infiltrated the neon-flashing big box cinema, purchased their offensively overpriced tickets, and watched *Gladiator* for the third time. But this third viewing is different from the others.

The first time, well—the first time requires no explanation. They'd seen Crowe in *L.A. Confidential* and *The Insider*, and they had seen him in the trailer for this latest film, so glistening with unalloyed manliness that they could almost smell him from their cushy stadium seats. So the first viewing was a given.

The second viewing took place the following week, motivated by reasons and longings similar to those that had compelled the first viewing. On that first Tuesday, the film had become an advertisement for itself. By the time Maximus had taken his first long look at the battlefield in the opening scene, the women knew that next week's "Girls' Tuesday" would again be devoted to this gladiatorial flesh carnival.

But this third viewing is another story entirely. They gave birth to tonight's mission during their usual after-show dessert following last week's movie. It started as a joke, but the more they talked about it, the more they meant it. Finally, they made a silly, but binding, pact that has led them to this moment: watches synchronized, hearts pounding, maps (sketched on napkins) ready, muscles twitching with anticipation. The credits have begun to roll, and the crowd is beginning to wander out of the theater in twos and threes.

Susan runs to Point A, a hidden corner outside the men's bathroom. Janice hangs back and tries to blend into the crowd. Sylvie darts left and starts an urgent discussion with an usher (Point B) about a fictional set of lost keys. As Janice's section of the outflowing movie crowd reaches Susan at Point A, Susan and Janice lunge right and together grab The Item. They try to move quickly and inconspicuously, but several other moviegoers have spotted the seizure. Sylvie and "the keys" are still monopolizing the usher's attention—is that a tear on her cheek? She's really playing it—but even so, Janice and Susan know they have to move The Item fast. Protecting it with their bodies as much as they can, they make eye contact and then a fast break. They hear only one irritated "Hey!" as they elbow through the crowd, and when they exit through the heavy glass doors Janice hears one woman ask, "Honey, where do you think they bought *that*?"

Hoisting The Item aloft in an awkward portage, the women sprint toward Sylvie's champagne-colored minivan (Point C), panting and still too genuinely exhilarated to laugh. Sylvie arrives a minute later, having feigned an embarrassed "discovery" of her keys in her purse. ("They get senile early, huh," the usher said to his pimply co-worker after she left.) Sylvie wants to pause and inspect The Item, but the two other women urge her, in the words of many a Hollywood fugitive before them, to "just get in and *drive*!"

Susan and Janice gingerly pass The Item into the back seat and everyone piles into the car. Once the doors are closed and the wheels are in motion, and they have made sure (all with a tinge of disappointment) that no theater employee is giving chase, raucous laughter and whoops of victory fill the van. Sylvie drives straight to Janice's place (speed limit all the way); no dessert tonight—they can't stop until the mission is totally complete.

They stumble, still weak with laughter, into Janice's small living room. They've come here because Janice is the only one of the three who's not married. She lives alone, so The Item is safe in her apartment. Once all are inside, the lights are on, and the curtains are drawn (they know this last paranoid measure is unnecessary, but it heightens the fun of their caper), they set The Item upright in the center of the room. Together they behold it and sigh deeply and theatrically, their sighs punctuated with laughter.

Before them stands a seven-and-a-half-foot cardboard cutout of

Russell Crowe

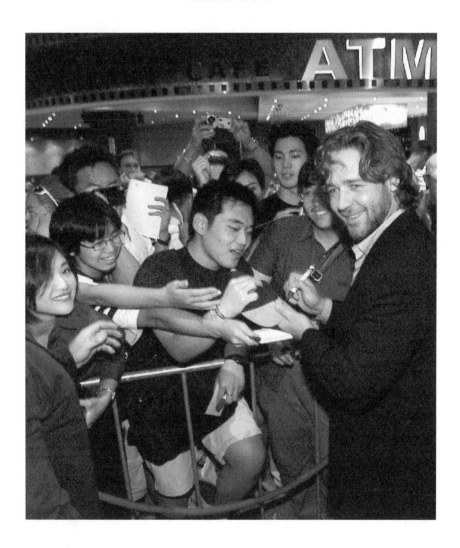

ALWAYS FRIENDLY WITH HIS FANS

LINDSAY MOLLER / NEWSPIX

Russell Crowe as Maximus—tawny, greased, leather clad: the first and best possible trophy in the history of the "Girls' Tuesday" crew.

"Ladies," Sylvie says with mock military seriousness, "a hero has risen."

It's 27 April 2000 in Rome, and Olivier Bonnard is surprised when he arrives at the bar where he is supposed to be interviewing the star of *Gladiator* and *The Insider*. He finds Russell Crowe already seated in a booth, looking slightly bored. Only slightly, mind you: not that particular stripe of Hollywood Bored that seems to shriek (even as it remains disdainfully silent), "Do you have any idea how many people would like to sleep with me, and consequently how many *far* more interesting things I could be doing at this moment?" Crowe just looks like a guy in a bar waiting for someone. A big guy, a powerful-looking guy who knows how to handle a horse and a broadsword at the same time, but just a guy nonetheless. Bonnard checks his watch, wanting to be absolutely certain before he approaches that he's not late. He's not.

He walks over to the booth where Crowe is seated and introduces himself. He has never been less certain of what to expect of an interview. By some accounts, Crowe is a borderline barbarian—an outback bruiser who would sooner take a swing at you and string you up using your own pants than answer even the most benign, unintrusive question. By other accounts, Crowe is a hugely talented (and intelligent) dramatic professional: a decent guy, but one so chock-full of integrity, diligence, and just plain seriousness about his work that he sometimes treats the glitter-obsessed media with . . . shall we say . . . hostility. Crowe looks up.

"How you doin', mate?" So far so good. Crowe seems affable. Bonnard sits down. The interview begins soon after Crowe has ordered a beer (not without first commenting that it's a fuckin' sin that you can't get a pint of VB—Victoria Bitter Ale—in these parts). Bonnard starts off with some easy questions, hoping to develop a bit of a rapport before he takes even the slightest risk. Crowe is remarkably agreeable. Their discussion meanders through the shooting of *Gladiator*, Crowe's impressions of Jeffrey Wigand, Michael Mann's efforts to convince Crowe to take the part of Maximus, Crowe's feelings about the issues *The Insider* raised about the power of Big Tobacco. As Crowe offers thoughts on this last subject, he lights up a cigarette. Without a word, Bonnard takes a long look at the smoldering tube. Crowe takes an equally long drag, ashes, and observes as he exhales, "I know. Isn't life full of irony?" Bonnard grins back. He likes this barbarian.

Where are the Beatles? Ladies and gentlemen, I ask you, *where are the Beatles*? Surely a crowd this wild, this desperate, this shrieking, this beside itself with anticipation can only be awaiting the arrival of the still baby-faced and bowl-headed Beatles. And yet surely the Beatles (let alone the still baby-faced and bowl-headed ones) can't be playing the outdoor venue behind Stubbs BBQ in

Austin, Texas on 4 August 2000. Who could have drawn this crowd, and whipped them into this state of agitation, if not those four all-surpassing legends of rock history?

Answer: A fifteen-year-old unknown folk-rock band from Australia, of course.

Yes, it is the hottest day of yet another sweltering summer in the Lone Star State, and Crowe-led Thirty Odd Foot of Grunts (you may, if you wish, refer to the band members simply as "The Grunts") is about to appear on this stage outside a barbecue restaurant here in, well, deep in the heart of Texas. And as the song about the heart of Texas tells us, the stars at night *are* big and bright here; or at least one star is. Russell Crowe is big enough to have required this performance to move to a larger venue after it became clear that the venue the band had originally planned on would not accommodate the throngs of fans who would show up, tickets or no, to behold the beefcake/*artiste* of the hour performing in his alternate medium. Once the change was made, despite the fact that the band allowed no publicity of the event and refused to issue press passes, this second location sold out in about the time it takes to say, "SWEET MOTHER OF GOD, RUSSELL CROWE IS COMING TO AUSTIN, TEXAS."

So here they all are, out back of Stubbs in the middle of summer. The heat is almost unbearable. It's made worse by the crowding, of course, as those who are about to be *one hundred and fifty feet away from Russell Crowe* push and struggle to increase the possibility that they might be *one hundred and forty feet away from Russell Crowe.*

PERFORMING WITH THIRTY ODD FOOT OF GRUNTS IN AUSTIN, TEXAS

KEYSTONE / SPLASH

Some of the quieter members of the audience remain perfectly still. These are the contemplative, bookish ones, who imagine (though they would never admit it) Crowe seeing them across the salmon-school crowd and saying, "You there, in the gleaming Keds, why do you not jostle and contend like these others? Why are you so serene, woman in the banana clip? Your difference must be a sign. Perhaps it is that you are to be my love." These quiet, still creatures also imagine their silent suffering in the scorching heat to be a kind of sacrifice for Crowe. Maybe he will see it in their eyes, as he starts to sing, that they have stood in this field behind Stubbs BBQ, amid thousands of crazed, celebrity-loving strangers, have become dehydrated and smelly and ruddy, have risked heatstroke and melanoma, all in his name. And he will want—he will need—to end their suffering.

OH! Here it comes now: AN END TO SUFFERING. The Grunts file casually onto the stage, Crowe assuming no special prominence except that, like every lead singer/guitar player, he heads downstage to face the crowd. The bandmates—Dean Cochran (guitar), Garth Adam (bass), Dave Kelly (drums), Stewart Kirwin (trumpet), and Dave Wilkins (guitar, vocals, tambourine)—seem to take the extra attention directed at Crowe in stride (if the screaming and reaching and rending of garments now taking place in the crowd with twice the intensity as before the stage filled up can be called "attention"). They're not idiots: they know that the band's recent rise to prominence is due largely to Crowe's new megastar status. But it's not hurting them any, and if they can keep doing their part musically, then playing to a sold-out venue in, of all places, Austin, Texas is all right by them. As bassist Garth Adam says to Lillian Vecchiarelli of *US Weekly*, "We all have day jobs. We are simply a group of friends who love music and enjoy playing. Years ago we made a promise to each other that we will get together at least once a year to play. What has happened in the meantime is that Russell has become very famous."

The band begins to play. Immediately, as in all situations such as this, part of the crowd is instantly rendered dumb with reverence for The Music, and another part of the crowd gets even wilder than they had been—perhaps wilder than they thought they could be. The opening tune is "Other Ways of Speaking," which, Crowe told interviewer Amy Reiter, is about "Finding somebody you think you could very easily fall in love with, and then realizing that they're playing for the other team." Some have suggested that the song was inspired by Crowe's relationship with Jodie Foster, one of the only people in Hollywood as fiercely protective of her personal privacy as Crowe is of his. No press to probe him for gossip tonight, though, as Crowe sings to an enthralled and reporter-free crowd.

As the raucous show wears on, the detritus of any truly manly band accumulates onstage: cigarette butts, empty beer cans, sweaty garments, and discarded towels. After a time, fans begin to ask—nay, *beg*—Crowe to bestow one of these amulets of ill health and rock and roll upon them. *Please, RUSSELLLLL!* Crowe ignores them at first. But as the pleading continues and increases in volume, Crowe, in disbelief and as if taking a dare, tosses a few of these objects into mob. He is shocked at the coyote-like struggle that ensues. Christ. "Get a life," he snorts, but with enough humor that none of the cigarette butt–grabbing women feels the need to cry.

The voracious hunger of this crowd for all things Russell is just one small indication of the change Crowe has experienced in his music career, which has in the past few years been totally eclipsed by his filmic fame. Garth Adam tells Vecchiarelli, "For us, mingling with people after performing, having close contact with fans has been very important. David, Dean and I hope we will be able to maintain this rapport. But for Russell, it is lost forever. And that saddens us and him."

The ruckus is overwhelming as a roomful of journalists maneuver for space and for the best view of the place where their prey will eventually be seated. Writers and photographers discuss his impending arrival, the dirt they expect to get, who will call the office, where they will go after this. Finally, Russell Crowe enters and sits down in a chair at the center of a long table. He does not look pleased. The room quiets down immediately and the questions begin. He answers most questions about his upcoming projects reluctantly. Occasionally, something seems to rub him the right way and he'll talk easily and articulately for a few minutes. Every once in a while, someone will be brave enough to ask about his love life. Those questions usually go over about as well as a bear baiting sideshow at a Humane Society fundraiser.

Eventually, some kid, clearly proud of his research, asks, "And Mr. Crowe, how is your band doing? Your band, Thirty Odd Foot of Grunge?" Some of the reporters don't spot their young peer's error. Others grin sadistically, waiting for Crowe to lay this guy low with sharp, news-making words that will shine forth from the pages of their respective publications. But Crowe is fairly gentle. Disdainful, but gentle. "You know, mate, you've really hit it. The reason we picked the name was so it'd be really unique, right? So people like you could remember it." The reporters laugh, partly to appease Crowe (about whom they have written so many scary stories by now that they have actually made themselves afraid of him), and partly out of awkwardness: Crowe is not happy to be here, and the tension generated by his obvious discontent spikes with each question posed.

Next, a British reporter who is partially hidden behind one of the large room's supporting columns catches Crowe's eye. Crowe nods, indicating that he will take the man's question. "Mr. Crowe, you've been developing a reputation over the past several years, with films such as *Gladiator* and *L.A. Confidential*, as a macho sort of person, a bit of a tough guy. One might look at your earlier work as presaging that image—might see a film such as *Romper Stomper*, for example, as a testosterone-driven hymn to brutality. But more than one critic has seen a certain homoerotic element in *Romper Stomper*, which would certainly introduce a twist to that tough-guy image. Would you care to comment on homoerotic undercurrents in any of your films?" Crowe stares back at the reporter, pretending to be dazed by the uncommon length of the reporter's pre-question speech. Then, in a moment of unexpected levity, he hammily shakes his head (apparently to clear it of the fog induced by the reporter's excessive verbiage) and begins to consider the question. "'Homo-erotic element,' right?" The actor strokes his chin as if deep in thought, and then affects a sudden brilliant realization: "Well, Christ, mate! You'd know more about all that than me, being English." A hearty chuckle runs through the room and the reporter nods good humoredly, acknowledging that Crowe's quip has effectively neutralized his question.

When the laughter has subsided, Crowe calls on a young female reporter who has had her hand raised for some time. The mood of the press conference is lighter now, as Crowe seems to have warmed up. It won't last. The reporter clears her throat. "Mr. Crowe, we know that when you're not working you live on your very isolated farm in Australia." Crowe brightens for a minute; it seems like this might be one of those questions that rub him the right way. Then the question goes slightly downhill. "And we know that you have associated yourself with more than one of the beautiful ladies in Hollywood, most recently Meg Ryan, who spends much of her time in California." He looks warily at the young journalist. Then it comes: "Would you ever consider a move to L.A. to improve your sex life?" It is immediately clear from Crowe's face that he has not just been rubbed the right way. His expression becomes deadly. He looks sideways, as if seeking an understanding face in which to seek sympathy for the tacky, invasive bullshit he has to put up with, but

CASTING A COY LOOK TO AN INTERVIEWER

BOB BARKER / NEWSPIX

no one's there. "Are you—" Crowe is genuinely flabbergasted. "Are you serious? I mean, that is sick, you know? I thought it was supposed to be about love." Crowe pauses, visibly upset. The room is silent, except for the incessant clicking of camera shutters. He looks back at the journalist. "You are . . . really terrible. You are." Crowe stands up and walks through a door near the front of the room. The offending reporter lowers her head. Russell Crowe, as they say, has left the building.

Crowe spots Dean Cochran from across the almost-empty bar. Cochran is already halfway through his first pint of Victoria Bitter Ale, and is staring into the remainder of the glass's contents with the melancholy that only a man staring at warming beer can display. He is also playing absently with the condensation that has accumulated on his thick cardboard coaster, sign number two that the laments of the world are indeed converging on the soul of one Dean Cochran tonight in Coff's Harbour. Crowe wanders over to the table and sits down across from his friend, having already ordered his own VB at the bar on his way.

Crowe is wearing sunglasses and a black baseball cap, two somewhat comforting, but usually useless, defenses against the public recognition and hounding that seem to increase weekly. It's a little better around here than it is in the U.S. Either he's familiar enough to people because of all the gigs Thirty Odd Foot of Grunts have played in this area over the years, or the locals are kind enough to give him a little breathing room, figuring he should be able to walk down the street in his own hometown (or the closest thing he has to a hometown). Crowe's not sure which of these factors makes the difference, and he doesn't much care. He's just grateful to have some peace.

Today, no one has looked twice as he has taken a seat across from his longtime bandmate and friend (he and Dean go back to the days of Roman Antix, Crowe's band in the early '80s, when Crowe wrote and recorded the uncannily prescient song, "I Wanna Be Like Marlon Brando"). "Tough day, mate?"

Cochran looks up; he hadn't even noticed when Crowe sat down. "Yeah. I'm all right. But this job can make you wonder about a fuck of a lot of stuff sometimes, you know? Depresses hell out of me sometimes, mate." Crowe nods silently. He admires Cochran's career as a social worker. All the members of the band have day jobs, although Crowe's is by far the most intrusive, with its travel demands and generally all-consuming nature. David Kelly does video editing, Garth Adam is in finance, and Cochran has been a social worker for years. His experiences in the field have sometimes contributed creative material to the band, as in the case of "The Legend of Barry Kable," which is about a homeless man Cochran took care of over a period of five years. But sometimes Cochran would rather not even discuss—let alone sing about—the small and large tragedies he witnesses every week, and such is the case tonight.

"Anything happen, mate?"

"Something is always happening. But fuck it for now. I can't think about it all the time. What did you come up with?" The two men have met to discuss possible titles for the album they recently recorded. Crowe said over the phone that he had a few ideas. Cochran says now that he had a couple, but decided they were shit. "So what are yours?"

"I got two front runners right now. First one's *Bastard Life*."

Cochran stops to consider for a second, then exhales thoughtfully, with puffed cheeks. "I like that one. That's really good. I think we should use it."

"Well hang on a sec, ya wanker, I've got another."

Cochran laughs for the first time today. "All right then, Mister Prolific Fucking Album-Namer, let it all out."

"*Clarity*."

A pause.

"Damn it, mate, I like that too. A lot. Maybe we should go with—oh, but we can't give up *Bastard Life*, that's gold. Shit, I don't know. Let's do both."

"Yeah, right," Crowe laughs, exhaling smoke.

Then Cochran looks up, entertaining the idea more seriously. "We could do it, though. *Bastard Life or Clarity*."

Crowe considers for a second. "Well, we'll have to clear it with the label." Both men laugh. Then they clink their glasses. Of course, there is no label. They produce and market all their own albums. In the early days, TOFOG was small enough that it could easily distribute its own records. The chances that anyone in Sweden or Japan would want an album by some obscure folk-rock band in Australia were . . . uh . . . not overwhelming, shall we say. The band did local tours that were reasonably well attended. They had a small but solid base of fans in Australia, they played their shows, were always writing new songs, and, in general, had a very viable small-time band going. But that had changed, just like everything else, with Crowe's rise to unthinkable global fame. Not only was it now certain that people in Sweden and Japan and a number of other far-flung locations would want CDs, but it also became clear that larger tours could be very successful. All of a sudden, Thirty Odd Foot of Grunts was a much bigger phenomenon than any of its members had anticipated. And then came the record companies.

Several big labels had expressed interest in the dumbstruck band, all obviously hoping to trade on the larger-than-life profile of its irresistible front man. Although the band had the same concerns about creative control that small bands generally have when they are suddenly thrust into the machinery that mass-produces popular culture, they were nevertheless interested in getting their music out to more people. So the record companies' attempts to woo them were not unwelcome. They even got close—very close—to signing with one of the big names. But Crowe had engineered a last-minute test of the company's dedication to the band itself, and the company had failed. Badly.

Most of the terms had been discussed, and both sides had agreed to the basic elements of the contract. Pens were practically in hand and dotted lines in view when Crowe mentioned that he'd like to release the next album, say, two months after his next movie came out, so it didn't get caught up in any of the publicity frenzy around the film. Of course, a publicity frenzy was exactly what the record company had been dreaming of. They wanted to release the album in conjunction with the film, and could not believe that Crowe would suggest otherwise. Needless to say, the marriage between band and business in this case did not even make it to the altar, let alone flourish into old age and obscene profit. So the band advertises and distributes their own CDs on the "gruntland" website and through a small, hands-off U.S. distributor. And they decide when to release their albums. And they decide which shows they will play. And they can name this new album any damn thing they want.

"*Bastard Life or Clarity*," muses Crowe. "Jesus—I'm twice as good as I thought."

"Shut up and order more beer, Shakespeare."

The photographer is pretty sure he is safe. He abandoned his car miles from here in some brush, and has kept up a good pace on foot. He traveled along the gravel road for about two hours before reaching the edge of the property, and then made his way across a grassy field (they must not farm this section of the land), staying as low as he could. He's almost certain his efforts at concealing himself were unnecessary, though. The Australian night is completely black: no stars, no moon, no light pollution from any nearby town. The farm lies in a valley between two long mountainous ridges; although there's life—communities, stores, traffic lights—on the other sides of these mountains, the valley that stretches out in either direction is totally devoid of any sign of human inhabitants. Except the farm itself, of course. And at the center of the farm, there is a single faint light that the reporter is trying to make his way toward, as quietly as possible. He thinks (he hopes) this is the Crowe household. If he could go home with shots of the farm and of Russell and the Crowes at home, even watching television or something horribly dull, his revenue for the year would be—well, markedly different from what it's ever been before.

As he begins to envision the look on his editor's face, his foot lands in a hole and his ankle is wrenched. He barely contains a girlish scream as he falls to the ground, managing to protect the camera as he falls, but not without the utterance of much unbecoming language. He's down for about five minutes, cursing and clutching the offended joint. He remembers from his high school basketball days that you should never take off your shoe: tighten it instead to contain the swelling. He does this with some difficulty, and decides that he can go on. After hoisting himself up with some self-pitying theatrics unwitnessed by any living thing (or so he imagines), he continues to lurch toward the light that signals Crowedom and, hence, professional success.

The house is actually nearer than it appears. He arrives in a cleared, yard-like area very soon after his fall. He is limping, but heartened by his sense that the luscious photographic fruit of his mission is at hand. Although he can't make out any of the house's detail because of the dark, he can tell that it's large. He heard that Crowe had it renovated when his career really picked up. ($20 million a movie, the guy makes. This operation may be a bit intrusive, the reporter thinks, but it's not so wrong for me to want a piece of this extremely profitable celebrity pie.)

The reporter crosses the yard silently (he is actually a little surprised that he hasn't been chased by dogs yet; he was prepared for that) and lies flat on his belly under some bushes beneath a lit window. He never realized his body could produce this much adrenaline in one go. What will he see when he rises to his feet next to the window? The parents? The brothers? A midnight snack? A game of chess? A servant? A mess?

These titillating musings are arrested by the sound of a *snip*. Then he feels a rubbing against his chest: before he realizes that the strap of his camera bag has been cut, and the device has been seized (the rubbing was the strap being dragged out from under him), his shoulder, too has been clutched. The reporter freezes, terrified.

"Get up," the voice that belongs to the hands says. The reporter complies. He turns to find the man himself emptying his camera of film, then going through the bag to look for other canisters. "So you wanted to meet me," Crowe says. The reporter says nothing. Crowe is not really asking anything—he is playing one of those games you see in movies where the killer lobs all kinds of banal questions at the victim before tearing out his heart and showing it to him while it's still beating. "Or maybe you wanted to meet my elderly mum. Is that it? You wanted to bother my mum?" The reporter remains silent. His ankle is throbbing. He decides at that moment that if he survives this he will become a nature photographer. Not even animals; only plants. Or maybe just rocks.

"Listen, mate. I really appreciate your taking time out to visit and all, but there are some things I should let you know before you try to do this all on your own again. Where'd you come through— there?" Crowe motions back to the field through which the reporter has just traveled. The reporter nods. "Yeah, that's what I thought. See, mate, that's not such a good route for visitors. You might not know this because you're from the city, right?" The reporter nods. "Well, we've got some extremely venomous snakes around here. And territorial, you know? You walk in some spot they've decided belongs to them, and, well, it's not so good for you. You know?" The reporter stares. "And then we've got these spiders. They're almost worse than the snakes because they can just get on you, you know, the way spiders do—they're pretty small little critters, really—but, of course, they're just as deadly as the snakes. So that can be not so good for you as well. Got it so far?" The reporter nods. "Yeah, and then we've got these strange little lizards. You've seen salamanders and geckos and that, mate?" The reporter nods. "Yeah, they're kind of cute, those little guys. But these other ones we've got 'round *here*, they're different. What they do, mate (it's strange; I can't quite figure out the evolutionary advantage of it, you know?) is they skitter up your body—up your leg, your side, maybe round your back a bit or your arm, over top your head, then down the other side. And they leave these little cuts with their claws wherever they step. They're sharp little buggers, really. You know?" The reporter nods. "But the thing is with these little cuts they give you. It's funny. I don't know how it works, exactly. I should look it up. See, it's just that they never . . . ever . . . ever . . . heal." The reporter stares. "So it's a weird spot we've got here. Especially for visitors, you know? See, we usually tell guests, people we've invited, about all this beforehand. And pick 'em up at the main road and all that, to be hospitable. But we didn't know you were coming." The reporter nods. "So I really do wish you luck in getting back to town. I'm sure you'll go as quickly as you can. And now you know for next time that you should ring first before coming out here, just to make sure we know to expect you, all right? Safer that way." Crowe hands the reporter his filmless camera, and gives his shoulder another painful squeeze. "See you, then." Crowe rounds the corner of the house and disappears. The reporter looks out across the field he has just crossed, and up at the black sky, and whimpers.

Is it the hips? Could it be the feet? How about the near-motionless upper body, rhythm plainly suffusing every cell of its arms, chest, and abdomen, yet not being allowed to erupt into the frenzy of which it is capable? (For now, that rhythm is being held—leashed—just below the surface of his skin.) "What . . ." the amazed veteran stunt man asks himself, "what *is* it that makes Russell Ira Crowe such a smoldering, room stoppingly hot dancer?" He cannot pinpoint the exact bodily source of this greatness.

After watching his magnetic colleague for another hour, though, the awestruck spectator has decided. It is not the hips, although the hips do move at once with the liquid smoothness of mercury on marble *and* the restrained precision of a dart thrower's wrist. It is not the feet, although the stunt man imagines one could place the fingers of a sleeping infant under Crowe's heels and hear not a cry, so weightlessly does the man appear to move on his scuffed soles. And it is not the upper body, still held spectacularly in check, despite its proximity to the fevered hips. No, the thing that makes Russell Crowe the kind of dancer who could—who just did—make a whole bar full of rhythmically astute Ecuadorians stop and stare, is his *mouth*.

And the elderly (but remarkably spry) woman with whom Crowe has been not so much cutting as burning a hole through the proverbial rug, knows it. She's been watching that mouth all night—the way it opens just slightly as Crowe moves forward, closes tight overtop of a furrowed chin when he steps back, the way it, every so often, offers about ten percent of the warmest smile she's never seen (the remaining ninety percent, not to mention a few celebratory kisses on her soft wrinkled cheek, is being held in reserve until the music stops and the bar explodes with applause and laughter and cries of *Que muchacho mas bueno para bailar!*). Oh, the rest of this splendid body has done just fine tonight—on this point there could not possibly be any debate—but it's the mouth that the woman will recall years from now when she and the others remember *los muchachos de Hollywood* who came to their bar one night for a drink and a dance.

A Life in Stories

Among *los muchachos de Hollywood* is the much-impressed stunt man who is now slapping Russell Crowe's drenched back and handing him a bottle of beer that's the color of apple juice. Crowe often develops a strong sense of camaraderie with the stunt people with whom he works, in large part because he frequently chooses to perform at least some of his own stunts, and so ends up trading tips and band-aids with the guys who do the dangerous stuff full time. Such was the case on the set of *Gladiator* and such is the case on this project. Beaming and breathing hard, Crowe sits down at his friends' table and takes a long sip from the bottle he's just been given.

The small group of colleagues assembled before him have made their way here, to this tiny one-room watering hole in the mountains of Ecuador, from Mount Chimborazol, the location where they've been filming *Proof of Life*. They decided to come and have a drink and meet the locals after Crowe had invited them (if his mockery of their nightly evacuation to the comfort and safety of a hotel in the city can be called an invitation) to spend a night in the mountains with him rather than returning to their usual urban lodging.

Crowe had insisted from the beginning on remaining near the site of filming because he preferred the peace of the mountains to the tumult of the city. So, he had fashioned a makeshift barbecue out of half an oil drum, acquired a trailer in which he could sleep, and had cheerfully (and perhaps a little smugly) stood at its threshold each evening and waved as the long caravan of his co-workers' cars pulled away. As usual, Crowe's attraction to untamed spaces was tinged with peril. Locals had warned the filmmakers of the dangers of the area, and the filmmakers had warned Crowe (almost hourly they had asked him to give up his one-man camping retreat, the tone of the warnings ranging from teasing to pleading—of course, no one dared to try scolding). Not only would there be kidnappers abroad in the night (Crowe had enjoyed more than one sardonic chuckle over the irony of suffering kidnapping threats while making a movie about a kidnapping), but the region in which they were filming was full of jungle cats that would no doubt find a man of Crowe's dimensions quite a satisfying meal. A little tough, perhaps—Crowe's physique in *Proof of Life* rivals *Gladiator* for its bulk and sinew—but quite a meal nonetheless. When asked by John Mosby of *Impact Magazine* about the danger he faced in roughing it alone each night in the wilds of Ecuador, cats and all, Crowe quipped characteristically, "I'll take the wildcats over the Ecuadorian drivers any day of the week."

But there is neither a hungry feline nor a reckless driver in sight tonight as Crowe and a handful of his usually hotel-dwelling colleagues laugh, drink, and, unexpectedly, dance at this tiny, but packed, local hangout. The stunt man who is now lighting Crowe's cigarette and ordering himself another beer certainly didn't know there would be dancing here. The place seemed too small. And even if someone had told him there would be dancing, he wouldn't have expected this infectious clothed orgy; usually when he thinks of dancing he thinks of his arthritic parents and of the vaguely depressing weddings of strangers. And even if someone had told him that there would be dancing at this matchbox of a bar, and even if someone had told him that the dancing would be the most spectacular, untouchingly erotic display he had ever seen, he would never have expected that Crowe could move his body like he just did. But then, surprise does seem to follow surprise when Crowe is around.

"Russell, look at your partner," the stunt man leans over to say. "She's still panting at the bar. You wore her out." Crowe turns to see the woman he was dancing with; she's looking at the ceiling and dabbing at her neck with a handkerchief. She's old enough to be his mother. "She's a genius," Crowe says as he motions to the single bartender to let him know that he will take care of the woman's tab. "Wonderful dancer."

"Never mind the partner, where did *you* learn to dance like that, Russell?" another cast member asks. "You been out here every night while we've been navel-gazing at the hotel?"

"Alex Crowe, mate. Taught me everything I know and a few things I forgot, no doubt. Here's to him." Crowe drinks. He recalls dance lessons in the living room with his dad, during his preadolescent years. His father would put on one of the few records they owned and they would dance—sometimes with Jocelyn, sometimes alone, always deep in concentration. He taught Russell the steps, the etiquette, how to lead but make it feel like no one's leading— like the bandleader, or the night, or God himself is actually calling the shots on the dance floor. But above all, Crowe's father taught him how to hear the music the way a painter sees a subject: by cutting out assumptions. To break the sound down into its most basic elements, understanding each individually. To blow the music apart in your head so you can absorb each bit into your body—this is the only way to really get the whole thing inside you. By the time Crowe hit high school, he was the smoothest mover on any floor he stood upon. Not that his tastes ran much to ballroom in those punk-blasted days.

At that age, Crowe might never have imagined that his training in and feel for dancing would prove an invaluable tool for his future acting career. As Crowe tells Mary Barrett, "one of the first things I want to do with actresses when we work together is manufacture a situation where we dance together. I can sense so many things when I am dancing—does she trust me? does she understand me? will she go around these scenes, this script with an open mind?" But tonight, the dancing has not been a fact-finding mission. It has been one hundred percent extracurricular. Crowe looks over at the woman at the bar. She's looking less flushed now, and is talking to the bartender about the night's unexpected events. She has never known a foreigner to be so skilled—to be capable of movement so fine. "Es Americano?" she asks of the man behind the bar, who shakes his head. Crowe overhears and calls over with a warm smile, "No, Señora." He turns around to his own table, which is surrounded largely by Americans. He makes a show of looking at each of them in turn with a playfully disgusted look on his face. "Fuck no, Señora," he groans, and takes another swig of his beer amid the scattered laughter and patriotic retorts of the table.

Russell Crowe is in the midst of an extremely serious meeting with the FBI. Although the actor has treated the kidnapping threats he has recently received in a joking, bravado-laden way during recent media interviews, the meeting currently underway in Crowe's hotel room is anything but light. Three agents arrived here about an hour ago, and since then the four men have gone over everything: from the usual procedures governing police treatment of kidnapping threats, to the likely motives and resources of the would-be kidnappers, to Crowe's concern for his parents and older brother, to whether, despite the threats, Crowe should attend the upcoming Golden Globe Awards ceremony (he has been nominated for an award for his performance in *Gladiator*). The group is leaning toward the decision that Crowe should attend the ceremony under heavy protection—Crowe doesn't want to go into hiding, and the FBI doesn't think there's much danger. Security will be scrupulous nevertheless, of course.

The meeting has been businesslike. The agents hadn't been certain what to expect of this celebrity supernova; like every other media-literate person in North America, the agents had heard wild and conflicting reports about the actor. They didn't know whether to expect a vain and overprivileged star, a crass and roguish brute, or a regular and now frightened person. Crowe has been ideal: professional, levelheaded, respectful of their expertise, and appreciative of their help. Now, as the four men are preparing to conclude their meeting, the man who seems to be the most senior of the agents pauses.

"Mr. Crowe, there's one more thing we'd like to discuss with you." Crowe had risen to see the agents out (understanding that surveillance of the hotel would continue), but now he nods seriously and sits back down, motioning for the agent to be seated again. The agent sits and clears his throat. "Mr. Crowe, well, as you know, we've had a great deal of experience with the kinds of people who are bothering you." Crowe nods. "We may not have encountered these particular individuals before, but we have something of a profile of the sorts of people who carry out these sorts of operations, particularly for ransom." Crowe is still attentive, although all this has already been covered in the earlier part of the meeting. "And, as you also know, we have done a considerable amount of research about you in order to be better able to help you and protect you at this time." Crowe gives a nod of thanks. The other two agents look on (their stances are broad, their hands hang folded in front of them, officially). They nod as their colleague proceeds; they know where he's headed.

"So what I'm trying to tell you, Mr. Crowe, is that we've assessed both sides of this situation fairly extensively and we've come to a conclusion." Pause. "We, as agents of the Federal Bureau of Investigation, believe that in all probability it is logistically beyond the power of the group or organization in question to get you to do any damn thing you don't want to do." The agents chuckle and nod. Crowe smiles broadly, appreciative both of the man's attempt at humor—after all, these guys look like people who iron their underwear—and at the playful reassurance he has offered.

**WITH BODYGUARDS/FBI IN THE BACKGROUND
AT THE 7TH ANNUAL SCREEN ACTORS GUILD AWARDS**

LISA O'CONNOR / KEYSTONE / ZUMA

"Right. I'll try to keep my own godlike power in mind as all this unfolds, mate." Everyone is eager to laugh after such a long, tense meeting, so they all do.

Director Taylor Hackford didn't even know until after they'd nearly finished shooting *Proof of Life*. He read of the affair (which had begun in Ecuador) in a London newspaper after he and his colleagues had traveled to England to film some final scenes. This was the first time Hackford learned that, during this project, Russell Crowe and Meg Ryan were falling in love and embarking on a relationship that was to last over half a year. When asked about his knowledge of the actors' being "linked," Hackford exclaimed that he hadn't had any idea—that both actors were totally professional—that it had all been completely discreet.

Upon reflection, it doesn't exactly boggle the mind that such a relationship might emerge. Ryan and Crowe certainly got along. And they are both—well, how to put it delicately? To begin with, Ryan never falls short of being approximately the cutest creature on earth. Never mind the obvious appeal of *Sleepless in Seattle* and *When Harry Met Sally*; ladies and gentlemen, that face almost made *City of Angels* bearable to watch. And as for Crowe, the lone-rogue-of-the-wilderness act was not without its charm. The makeshift barbecue? Winsome. The night of dancing? Gorgeous. Doing his own stunts for the sake of (isn't this a bad word in Hollywood) *authenticity*? Completely irresistible. I mean, imagine the conversation Crowe must have had with friend Tom Cruise when he called to talk to Cruise about whether he should refuse to allow a stunt man to do the scene in which Crowe's character hangs by his fingertips from a helicopter in flight. (Cruise was the expert, since he had performed an almost identical stunt in *Mission: Impossible*.) Did the talk go something like . . .

> "So, like, how dangerous is it, mate?"
> "Pretty dangerous."
> "But it looks good?"
> "Looks great."
> "With the fingertips?"
> "Fingertips. And the helicopter."
> "Yeah. 'Course. Sweet."

In short, the man's cool is beyond dispute.

So, then, it makes sense that these two immensely attractive individuals, provided they found themselves in agreement on a few fundamentals (Crest vs. Colgate, mountains vs. ocean, smooth vs. crunchy—that sort of thing), might find themselves desirous of some shared quality time. Indeed, as Sarah Saffian revealed in *US Weekly*, at one point Hackford felt the match was so right that he exclaimed, "They were fantastic together. They didn't know each other before, and then kaboom. That's how relationships are formed, and hopefully it'll last forever."

But as Hackford's mental wheels continued to turn, he began to wonder whether shared quality time is really where it ended. Maybe the romance had broader implications. Maybe it (and all the accompanying media murmurs: "It's hot!" "It's not." "Marriage!" "Rocks.") was partially responsible for *Proof of Life's* disappointing box office showing.

But then again, maybe not. "I think Taylor is being impolite, impolitic and imbecilic by saying that," Crowe retorted to a scrum of journalists, as reported by *iWon*. "I think you will see that the *Proof of Life* box office, when it's not such a family-oriented time as Christmas, will be much higher. What we know, personally, is that we put as much effort into the process as possible and are pleased with the outcome." Impolite, impolitic, and imbecilic? Hmmm. Not bad vocab for a lone-rogue-of-the-wilderness sort.

Feedback squeals for a second from the speakers stationed around the room as the band, Thirty Odd Foot of Grunts, does a second quick sound check before they start. The band's front man, none other than the versatile and virtuosic Russell I. Crowe, has been called away to answer what a reporter insists will be only a very few questions about tonight's event. Crowe assents, seeing the importance of discussing the fundraiser with the press, and having been assured that the interview will not wander into other, shall we say, less civic-minded territory.

The journalist asks what drew Crowe and his band to tonight's benefit. The gala in Milan is being hosted by designer Giorgio Armani and ex-duchess Sarah Ferguson to raise money for "Children in Crisis," a charity Ferguson founded in 1983 after a trip to Poland during which she was shocked by her encounters with children in extreme poverty.

Upon being asked by Michael Quintanilla, a fashion reporter from the *Los Angeles Times*, to comment on the night's glamorous hosts, Crowe praises Armani's designs, in which Crowe has graced the Dorothy Chandler Pavilion on more than one occasion: "his clothes fit men, they're not for the boys. He makes clothes that are classic and for men with deep voices." Crowe goes on to explain that he and The Grunts agreed right away to play tonight's show because they believe strongly in the work of Ferguson's "Children in Crisis." Of course, there's not much else one *can* say. ("Oh, well, I don't go in for kids much. They're just so needy, you know? Espe-*ci*ally the ones in crisis.")

But Crowe's statement of praise for the organization seems genuine—not just empty star-at-a-fundraiser talk. ("Yes, I donated an autographed stiletto heel that I wore to a party at Sundance, Mary. Brad, sweetheart, what did it go for? . . . *No!* Oh, God, Mary, it went for $8,500. I'm just so glad I could help, because you know, bedwetting is an issue that affects so many of our precious children and this organization is just doing some remarkable work.")

Crowe's record with children bears up the seeming earnestness of his support for Ferguson's project. Not only does he often speak of himself as a somewhat childish character—he described Jodie Foster as the perfect date for him at the 2001 Golden Globe awards because she let him be as goofy as he wanted to be—but he also

ESCORTING JODIE FOSTER AT THE GOLDEN GLOBES

ROSE PROUSER / REUTERS / GETTY IMAGES

seems to have a certain rapport with that other kind of child, the kind that doesn't inhabit a 6-foot, 200-pound frame. Crowe is a favorite with close friend Jodie Foster's son, Charlie, and has always delighted in spending time with his now teenaged niece whom he teases endlessly as though he were a kid brother, not a grown uncle. At recent awards ceremonies he has gravitated toward younger attendees; and though (*Gladiator* co-star) Joaquin Phoenix and (*Billy Elliot* star) Jamie Bell hardly qualify as children any longer, they are the closest thing to younger brothers (with all the goofing-around capabilities that title implies) Crowe is likely to find at such events.

Crowe speaks of his own childhood with what seems to be affection for his younger self. He describes his boundless confidence in the period when he first began to act to Chuck Arnold: "Even at six, I would look at the 28-year-old guy playing the war veteran in a film and tell my parents, 'I don't know why the director doesn't see me in that role. I might be a little short, but I can do it.'" And of his motivation to start along the dramatic path that would eventually see him asking $20 million per picture, he tells Jill Derryberry, "It became apparent to me that acting was a really fun thing to do. And when you're six years old and three feet tall, that's a good enough damn reason."

Much as he has shown love for the innocent and silly sides of kids (and of himself), Crowe also takes the state of childhood very seriously. He was once offered the role of the menacing father in the film adaptation of Dorothy Alison's *Bastard Out of Carolina*. Though there was no doubt that the film was of the serious sort—

serious being the kind of work Crowe has tried to pursue through-out his career—and that Crowe could have used the work and exposure that accepting the role would have provided, he refused the part because he was unwilling to perform the film's disturbing scenes of child abuse. So, yeah. You could say that Crowe has a certain sympathy with the little people of the world.

Interview complete, Crowe is heading back to the stage to begin performing with the band, which is now ready to start its set. The audience, full of actors and local fashion scenesters, greets The Grunts warmly. Crowe looks out over the crowd and remarks, "This is the best-looking audience we've ever played before." The beautiful people laugh. ("Who? Us?") Then, suddenly, Crowe turns from affable charity gala–attending celebrity to sexy, hard-edged rock star. "We're gonna sing for Sarah," he cries into the microphone as the band breaks into "Somebody Else's Princess," a tune from their album *Bastard Life or Clarity*. The song is about a man's longing for a woman who, coincidentally, has strawberry hair and blue eyes.

Ppt. Cccchhhhkk. Ppt. Whirrrrrrr. That sound? Oh, that's just the rumor mill sputtering to life.

The bastard. The shameless, shit-eating bastard, Crowe thinks. And to think that such a small man should be allotted, by the hand of fate, such a lovely suit as the one he's wearing tonight. Of course, everyone here is dressed well—lavishly, even. That's no crime. It's just that in this particular case, looking good actually seems a moral misstep—a deceit. Of course, this guy is not the only slimy player Crowe has met since he's been working in Hollywood, but there's something about the tension between his fine suit and his fetid, worm-eaten soul that has really gotten under Crowe's skin.

The two men—Russell Crowe and director Lawrence Kasdan— have been mingling at the Directors Guild Awards, where Crowe has been receiving sidelong glances of admiration all night. Although Ridley Scott was edged out in the Best Director category by Ang Lee (for *Crouching Tiger, Hidden Dragon*), the likelihood of Crowe's picking up an Oscar later this year for his performance in *Gladiator* remains undiminished. And it's more than just the Oscar that makes Crowe seem to hover a couple of inches above the floor tonight. Everyone in the room understands that Crowe has *arrived* in a way that many—not just many average people, but many of these, the titans of Tinsel Town—never will. He has been at the center of the latest Ridley Scott/Dreamworks blockbuster, number thirty-four in the one hundred highest-grossing films of all time. He has slowly and doggedly created a resume of unwavering quality, waiting patiently for recognition that the whole world suddenly seems eager to lavish upon him. He has openly scoffed at the vanity and artifice of the Hollywood lifers, and people have *loved* him for it. Simply put, Crowe is at the top of the heap, on his own terms, and every-one knows it.

Though he does his best not to believe in "the game" itself, Crowe is not unaware of the fact that whatever strange sport governs this town, he seems to be winning. And so he is not the least bit confused by the fact that Lawrence Kasdan, a man who, a few years ago, wouldn't even let Crowe put two sentences together in his presence, has just approached him, eager to talk. The two men's eyes had met across a few tables, and Kasdan had raised his chin and his eyebrows, as if to say, "Hang on, buddy, I see you over there and I'm on my way."

As Kasdan approached, Crowe conjured in his memory the time he had met the director a few years (not to mention a few critically acclaimed films) ago. Crowe had been trying to describe to the director some ideas he had had about a potential project, and had suddenly noticed that Kasdan was staring right through him—that mentally, Kasdan was somewhere else entirely and, worse, that he wasn't even trying to *look* like he was giving Crowe the time of day. The director, Crowe had realized bitterly at the time, was going almost out of his way to signal to the young Australian that his ideas didn't count—that he was not in The Rolodex and therefore was not worth the time it would have taken to have that discussion. Crowe has not forgotten this early encounter, but apparently Kasdan has.

He has just eased up beside Crowe and, with a great warm grin and a readily offered handshake, said, "Great speech, Russell. We were eating it up! You know, I'm really impressed with your approach to the roles you've been taking recently—impressive intensity. You and I really should meet . . ." Crowe stares at the man for about seven seconds, giving him a chance to realize his error and retreat.

But Kasdan just stands and grins, not comprehending the meaning of Crowe's silent, stony gaze.

"Actually, Larry, we have met. Don't you remember?" Kasdan turns down the corners of his mouth, making a show of scanning through recent star encounters in his head. Coming up empty, he shakes his head and grins again, waiting for Crowe to acknowledge a mistake. But Crowe is not mistaken. "Yes, we met. And as a matter of fact, I didn't find you terribly impressive as a human being, which you will understand if you ever find yourself able to call to mind the meeting in which you couldn't bring yourself to pay attention to me for twelve seconds at a stretch. So if you'll excuse me."

Crowe brushes past Kasdan before the director can even perceive the self-inflicted gunshot wound that has just metaphorically opened up in the center of his foot. Crowe strides away through the chatting groups of ceremony attendees, many of whom vie to catch his eye in hopes of striking up a conversation. As he moves through the crowd, he gives a quiet high-five to his former self, the struggling would-be star who lived for years on cigarettes and fried rice in downtown Sydney. That, my friend, Crowe remarks to his internal alter-ego, was sweet as a biscuit. Don't you agree?

Russell Crowe takes a long look at himself in the room's full-length mirror. He has just pulled on the jacket of his Edwardian-style Armani suit (for men with deep voices, remember—there is little danger that Crowe and Leo will accidentally appear in the same outfit tonight). He shrugs and the jacket falls into place over his broad frame. He is dressed. For tonight.

There is no prom king giddiness here, despite the dashing attire the man has just donned, and despite the lavish celebration that is to come. Crowe is alone and he is solemn. This is not just another party. It is not even just another awards ceremony. It is the zenith of his career to date. There's something admirable in Crowe's honesty about the fact that the night—as in The Night; as in the Dorothy Chandler Pavilion and Joan Rivers making nasty cracks about Bjork in a swan dress—matters deeply to him. He displays none of that false air of nonchalance that so many of his peers try to conjure. As ever, Russell Crowe is not afraid to want something, and not afraid to let it show. He recognizes the Oscar as "the ultimate peer-based accolade," in his words to Garth Pearce of the *London Sunday Times*, and says to a press conference early in the month, "I don't have any funny line. I don't have a cynical opinion on it. I'm really appreciative and very thankful."

Of course, he wants to win. But if he doesn't . . . well, he's known harder knocks. After all, work is work and just to be nominated is a great—but there isn't time for this sort of talk. Crowe has got to hurry up and he is still far from equipped for the evening. Call it superstition, call it sentimentality, call it adding five pounds to the weight of his outfit, but Crowe has a number of charms and talismans to place on his person.

First, there is the plastic toy from Charlie. Charlie being Charlie Foster, son of Jodie Foster and serious buddy of Russell Crowe.

Crowe has laughed off, with remarkable grace and patience, reporters' suggestions that he might have sired young Charlie. He makes no bones, though, about the fact that he and the kid get along. Evidence of the friendship is at present slipping into Crowe's pants' pocket; Charlie gave him this little toy as a token of support on Crowe's big night, and Crowe would not think of leaving it behind. So, charm number one is in place.

Charm number two is similarly sweet, if slightly more lasting than Charlie's small plastic figure. It is a silver cross given to Crowe by Meg Ryan, and inscribed with a passage from one of Crowe's favorite poems. The poem is "Clancy of the Overflow," an Australian classic written by Banjo Paterson in the late 1880s. Given Crowe's deep attachment to his rural home, it is not difficult to see why the poem would resonate with him:

> I had written him a letter which I had, for want of better
> Knowledge, sent to where I met him down the Lachlan, years ago,
> He was shearing when I knew him, so I sent the letter to him,
> Just "on spec," addressed as follows, "Clancy, of The Overflow."

> And an answer came directed in a writing unexpected,
> (And I think the same was written with a thumb-nail dipped in tar)
> Twas his shearing mate who wrote it, and verbatim I will quote it:
> "Clancy's gone to Queensland droving, and we don't know where he are."

> In my wild erratic fancy visions come to me of Clancy
> Gone a-droving "down the Cooper" where the Western drovers go;
> As the stock are slowly stringing, Clancy rides behind them singing,
> For the drover's life has pleasures that the townsfolk never know.

And the bush hath friends to meet him, and their kindly voices greet him
In the murmur of the breezes and the river on its bars,
And he sees the vision splendid of the sunlit plains extended,
And at night the wond'rous glory of the everlasting stars.

I am sitting in my dingy little office, where a stingy
Ray of sunlight struggles feebly down between the houses tall,
And the foetid air and gritty of the dusty, dirty city
Through the open window floating, spreads its foulness over all

And in place of lowing cattle, I can hear the fiendish rattle
Of the tramways and the buses making hurry down the street,
And the language uninviting of the gutter children fighting,
Comes fitfully and faintly through the ceaseless tramp of feet.

And the hurrying people daunt me, and their pallid faces haunt me
As they shoulder one another in their rush and nervous haste,
With their eager eyes and greedy, and their stunted forms and weedy,
For townsfolk have no time to grow, they have no time to waste.

And I somehow rather fancy that I'd like to change with Clancy,
Like to take a turn at droving where the seasons come and go,
While he faced the round eternal of the cash-book and the journal—
But I doubt he'd suit the office, Clancy, of "The Overflow."

The lines Ryan has chosen, which Crowe read to a reporter on Oscar night, are these: "and he sees the vision splendid of the sunlit plains extended / and at night the wondrous glory of the everlasting stars." Crowe silently rereads (for the thousandth time) the inscription, and slips the silver cross into the pocket opposite the one in which Charlie's offering is stowed.

Now he pulls his jacket straight again and reaches for a velvet box on the dresser to his left. He opens it to find a gold disc attached to a red ribbon. He fingers the medal gently, and removes it from the box. With the greatest care, he affixes the piece to the right breast of his jacket. His hands drop to his sides and he beholds himself, sixteen years after his grandfather's death, wearing that man's medal signifying his status as a Member of the Order of the British Empire.

Crowe's maternal grandfather, Stan Wemyss, had been a heroic war cinematographer. Working for New Zealand's National Film Unit during the Second World War, Wemyss was often close to action, fired upon as he documented the events of the war. The MBE was bestowed upon him by Queen Elizabeth II in recognition of his artistry and bravery. Wemyss didn't like to wear the medal that Crowe has just placed on his own chest, but Crowe thinks he would approve tonight. After all, this is not just any black tie occasion. This is the night that Crowe is to be honored (to what extent he does not yet know) by the film industry; it's only right that this symbol of his grandfather's valiant contributions to the form should get to spend the evening in the spotlight with the night's soon-to-be-anointed hero.

When he was young, Russell had seen his grandfather's work in film as something like alchemy: mysterious and romantic, but at the same time highly technical, demanding great skill. Stan had kept some editing equipment and cameras in the basement, and when Russell would follow him down into the studio ("covert under-ground laboratory" seemed a more appropriate name) it would be like descending into the Hall of Justice or some other clandestine headquarters where the heroes of the world dream up solutions to our most pressing problems, using staggering ingenuity and out-of-this-world know-how. Of course, on any given day, Stan Wemyss would probably have insisted modestly that what he was doing had absolutely nothing to do with the world's most pressing problems. But the fact of Wemyss's personal history of wartime bravery made Russell regard all his grandfather's actions and projects as having great moral consequence. Besides, even under the age of ten, Crowe knew a hero when he saw one.

When Crowe got older, it became clear that his grandfather's experience in the war, though frequently interwoven with clicking film, was hardly the stuff of movies. Well, maybe the stuff of the nuanced, conflicted movies Crowe would someday make, but not of the kind in which righteous soldiers either died on the battlefield or returned home to lives of quiet satisfaction at their victory over the forces of evil. Crowe began to realize just how traumatized his grandfather had been—had realized just how far the character of Wemyss's life after the war had been from "quiet satisfaction"— when grandfather had visited grandson in Sydney at a time when Crowe was still struggling to keep body and soul together on a sparse and erratic acting income. Wemyss was planning to take Crowe out to dinner, and Crowe suggested a Japanese restaurant he used to walk by, and peer into with longing, every day. It seemed at the time like a wonderful indulgence, but it turned out to be "a rotten choice," as he told Adam Sherwin. Even the smell of soy sauce brought

WITH HIS CRICKET CHAMP COUSINS JEFF AND MARTIN CROWE

OCEANIA NEWS AND FEATURES

Wemyss back to some interior battlefield. He became so lost in his own troubled thoughts that he didn't even manage to tell Crowe what he had come to tell him: that he was dying.

Recalling his sad mistake of so many years ago, Crowe reaches up to his chest under the pretense of straightening the medal. The medal does not need straightening. He just wants to touch it again.

There is no medal on Crowe's chest to signify the second hero that will accompany him to the podium tonight after his name is announced. But then, if anyone should require tangible evidence of Crowe's late uncle David Crowe, there are plenty of photos of him on the set of *Gladiator*, the film for which Crowe will be recognized tonight. About a year ago, 12 May 2000, David Crowe died of cancer. But long before then, when he had been well enough to travel and laugh and play cricket, David and sons Martin and Jeff (both world-class cricketers) had traveled to Malta to visit Russell on the set of *Gladiator*. Not only did the men form a Crowe-centered cricket team (CCC, or Crowe's Cricketing Cronies) that faced off against (and just barely lost to) a local team from the Marsa Sports and Country Club, but David and company were invited, thanks to Russell, to serve as stand-in senators in some of the coliseum scenes. As it turned out, the shots couldn't be squeezed in and the Crowes didn't even make it as far as the cutting room—but Dave exulted in the experience nevertheless, remarking with humble excitement, "As a frustrated thespian I am thrilled to just watch and mingle."

David and Russell had been close throughout Russell's life. And though his uncle witnessed more of Russell's success than had his grandfather, who died while Russell was still poor and unknown, Crowe regrets that his uncle Dave can't see him tonight—at the pinnacle of his career (so far) and at the culmination of the filming process in which Dave had so delighted.

But there's not much time left for reflection. Crowe takes a deep breath and a final inventory of the things he is carrying. He turns and strides away from the mirror.

The solemnity with which Crowe has invested the evening is not destined to last. Soon enough, our noble hero will be thrust into the idiot airs of his industry. He can handle a broadsword and wrestle a tiger, but how to honorably repel attacks of the kind he will weather tonight? He reaches the battlefield and meets not spiked weapons and flaring equine nostrils, but rather Joan Rivers offering a catty little critique (to a mere billion of her most intimate confidants) of Crowe's personal scent. Our warrior presses forward, eyes on the horizon, ignoring the petty indignities that accompany widespread renown. But upon crossing the moat of flashbulbs and microphones, upon dexterously navigating the red carpet (which, our hero suspects, has earned its hue by cradling the broken, bleeding bodies of those who have traveled this path before him), upon making his way into the very center of the arena, he meets not savage bestial foes or a leering, malevolent emperor; instead, he finds Steve Martin making cracks of a roughly "Yo Mama" quality on the subject of Crowe's supposed philandering. Our hero is gravely wounded. He had not expected such warfare mean and low. His weapons are from another time—his character forged in a fire far distant. And yet, ladies and gentlemen, and yet . . . *He wins.*

Works Consulted

Anidjar, Patrick. "Russell Crowe's Quiet Strength Wins an Oscar." *Agence France Presse* 26 Mar. 2001.

Archer, Michael. "Crowe's Talent, Drive Catapult Career." *Daily Variety* Mar. 7.

Arnold, Chuck. "Manifest Destiny." *People* 6 Oct. 1997.

Aurelius, Marcus. *Meditations*. New York: Washington Square, 1964.

Bain, Charlie. "Gladiator Star Russell Gets Shirty." *The Mirror* 26 Mar. 2001.

Barrett, Mary. "Tough Guy, Soft Heart." *Real Magazine* 3-16 Apr. 2001.

Bonnard, Olivier. "Birth of a Hero." *Le Nouveau Cinema* Mar. 2000. http://www.geocities.com/Hollywood/Cinema/1501/.

Bradley, David. "The Big Somewhere with Russell Crowe." *Celluloid Interview* 28 Dec. 1997. http://www.thei.aust.com/film97/cellincrowe.html.

Brown, Jeremy K. "Russell Crowe." *Current Biography* 61.5 (2000).

Chen, Joie, et al. "Russell Crowe Discusses Kidnapping Plot Against Him." *CNN News Site 16:00* 9 Mar. 2001. Transcript 01030905v76.

Craig, Alex. "Who You Looking At?" *HQ* June 2000.

Crowe, Dave. "CCC Crowe XI." *Maximum Russell Crowe* June 1999. http://www.geocities.com/Hollywood/Cinema/1501/maxcrowe_relative.html.

——. "A Day on the Set." *Maximum Russell Crowe* June 1999. http://www.geocities.com/Hollywood/Cinema/1501/maxcrowe_relative.html.

——. "Dinner With Derek." *Maximum Russell Crowe* July 1999. http://www.geocities.com/Hollywood/Cinema/1501/maxcrowe_relative.html.

——. "Down to His Fingertips." *Maximum Russell Crowe* Feb. 1999. http://www.geocities.com/Hollywood/Cinema/1501/maxcrowe_relative.html.

"Crowe Hits Out at 'Imbecilic' Criticism of Romance." *iWon* 24 Feb. 2001.

"Crowe's Upward Flight." *BBC News Online* 23 Feb. 2001.

"Crowe Wins Best Actor Oscar." *United Press International* 26 Mar. 2001.

Cruz, Clarissa. "Russell Crowe." *Entertainment Weekly* 22-29 Dec. 2000.

Curry, Shayne and Kim Purdy. "As the Crowe Flies Home." *Sunday Star-Times* [Auckland] 7 May 2000.

Dargis, Manhola. "Russell Crowe's Special Brand of Masculinity." *New York Times* 4 Mar. 2001.

Davey, Edmund and Jo Max. "Go Russ Go!" *Australian Women's Weekly* May 2001.

Derryberry, Jill. "Russell Crowe." *Interview* Aug. 1995.

DeSouza, John. "Crowe Confidential." *Happening* Nov. 1997. http://happening. com.sg/film/features/1997/november/crowe/.

Diamond, Jamie. "Straight out of Australia, to L.A." *New York Times* 26 Mar. 1995.

Dinglasan, Francesca. "Something to Crowe About." *Box Office Online* Aug. 1999.

Dwyer, Graham. "From Gladiator to Negotiator." *Daily Yomiuri* 15 Mar. 2001.

Dwyer, Michael. "Six Odd Foot of Grunt." *Sunday Age* 18 Feb. 2001.

Eliezer, Christie. "Crowe's Feat." *Sain Magazine* Feb. 2001

"Film Star Checks on Ill Uncle." *Press* [Christchurch] 8 May 2000.

Fink, Mitchell and Lauren Rubin. "Defeated Gladiator Licks His Wounds." *Daily News* [New York] 23 Jan. 2001.

"*Gladiator* Heartthrob and Oscar Nominee Russell Crowe Talks about *Proof of Life* and Leading Lady Meg Ryan." *Hello! Magazine* 26 Feb. 2001.

"'Gladiator' Russell Crowe Is Seriously Single-Minded." *Florida Times-Union* 5 May 2000.

Hardy, Morris. "Who's Flying Off with Our Crowe Pics?" *Mirror* 26 June 2000.

Hobson, Louis B.. "Here's the Inside Scoop: Crowe Won't Win an Oscar." *Sun* [Edmonton] 14 Mar. 2000.

Hoffman, Bill. "Kidnappers Planned to Maim Actor Crowe: Cops." *New York Post* 19 Mar. 2001.

Howell, Peter. "Toga! Toga! Toga!" *Toronto Star* 24 Mar. 2001.

Jones, Adam. "Tobacco Firm Refuses to Crowe." *Times* [London]. 27 Mar. 2001.

Kagan, Daryn, et al. "Russell Crowe Stalked for Kidnapping." *CNN Live This Morning 9:00* 7 Mar. 2001. Transcript 01030723V74.

Kelly, Christopher. "The Kidnapping Plot Thickens; Die, Gladiator, Die!" *Fort Worth Star-Telegram* 9 Mar. 2001.

Kirkland, Bruce. "Backstage with Crowe." *Sun* [Edmonton] 27 Mar. 2001.

Koha, Nui Te. "Crowe at the Crossroads." *Weekend Magazine* 17 Feb. 2001.

Laufer, Bonnie. "Relishing His Role as the Greatest Hero of the Empire." *Tribute* June 2000.

Lines, Andy. "The Oscars 2001: An Epic Night: Don't Crowe There, Steve." *Mirror* 27 Mar. 2001.

——. "The Oscars 2001: An Epic Night: The Gladioscar; Victor Crowe Pays Tribute to His War Hero Grandfather." *Mirror* 27 Mar. 2001.

Linley, Julian. "The Crowe Road to Hollywood." *Heat* 24-30 June 2000.

Lowe, Andy. "Man of the Year: Russell Crowe." *Total Film* Jan. 2001.

Major, Wade. Press Conference 12 Mar. 2000. http://www.geocities.com/Hollywood/Cinema/1501/.

"The Making of *The Quick and the Dead*." *The Quick and the Dead Unofficial Web Page* http://www.thequickandthedead.net/rc.html June 2001.

Mcpherson, Lynn. "Kidnappers Planned to Cut Crowe's Fingers Off; Police Catch Gang Suspect." *Sunday Mail* 18 Mar. 2001.

Methven, Nicola. "Nudiator; Crowe Learns Ropes As a Bareback Rider." *Mirror* 16 Dec. 2000.

Meyer, Josh. "FBI Probing Alleged Plot to Kidnap Actor Crowe." *Los Angeles Times* 7 May 2001.

Mosby, John. "Something to Crowe About?" *Impact Magazine* May 2001.

Nashawaty, Chris. "Chairman of the Sword." *Entertainment Weekly* 12 May 2000.

Nason, Pat. "Profile of Oscar Nominee Russell Crowe." *United Press International* 25 Mar. 2001.

Nuwar, Sara. "From Small Beginnings to Oscar Winner." *Press Association Newsfile* 26 Mar. 2001.

"Oscar Won't Change Me, Says Crowe." *AAP Newsfeed* 27 Mar. 2001.

Palmer, Martyn. "Grrr..." *Empire Magazine* June 2000. www.geocities.com/jcimelli/empirejune2000.html

Paget, Dale. "Crowe Unconcerned Over Security Threat at Oscars." *AAP Newsfeed* 26 Mar. 2001.

Paterson, Banjo. "Clancy of the Overflow." www.middlemiss.org/lit/poetry/clancy.html

Pearce, Garth. "'One of the Most Intelligent Actors Around': Russell Crowe, the Outsider." *Times* [London] 5 Mar. 2000.

Powers, John. "The Bad and the Beautiful." *Vogue* Feb. 2000.

Quintanilla, Michael. "Swords and Sandals? No, Songs and Armani." *Los Angeles Times* 2 Mar. 2001.

Rafferty, Terrence. "Russell Crowe: Film Actor." *GQ* Nov. 2000.

"Rock and Crowe." *The Gold Coast Bulletin* 31 Dec. 1998.

Rofail, Nadine. "Good Omen for Aussie Oscar Nominee." *AAP Newsfeed* 24 Mar. 2001.

Rohrer, Trish Deitch. "Man on Fire." *GQ* Mar. 1999.

Roman, Shari. "Crowe's Feat." *Flaunt* May 2000.

"Russell Crowe, It's Anyone's Bet." *Studio* http://www.geocities.com/Hollywood/Cinema/1501/.

"Russell Crowe, Man of Many Sides." *New York Times* 18 Mar. 2001.

"Russell Crowe Will Throw His Hat into Three Rings." *San Diego Union-Tribune* 6 Feb. 2000.

Saffian, Sarah. "Russell Crowe: Shy Guy, Sexy Rebel." *US Weekly* 5 Feb. 2001.

Savlov, Marc. "Gruntwork." *The Austin Chronicle* Aug. 2000.

Sherwin, Adam. "Crowe Displays Family Pride." *Times* [London] 27 Mar. 2001.

Slee, Amruta. "An Australian Actor Tries Life As a Neo-Nazi Punk." *New York Times* 6 June 1993.

"Special Moment for Crowe Widow During Oscar Speech." *Agence France Presse* 27 Mar. 2001.

Standora, Leo. "*Gladiator* Crowe Kidnap Threat, FBI Says." *Daily News* [New York] 7 Mar. 2001.

"Stardom Doesn't Alter Russell Crowe's Nature." *The Florida Times-Union* [Jacksonville] 15 Dec 2000.

Stavrinos, Anthony. "Crowe Just One of the Boys Down at His Local." *AAP Newsfeed* 26 Mar. 2001.

Stein, Ruthe. "Pretty Face, *Beautiful Mind*." *San Francisco Chronicle* 16 Mar. 2001.

"Sweet Revenge: For Russell Crowe, Revenge Is Sweet." *Canoe* http://www.the-crowes-perch.com/articles/crowe_facts_canoe.htm.

Sylvester, Sherry. "When Acting Bug Bit, Some Stars' Parents Howled." *CNN Showbiz Today Reports* 22 Mar. 2001.

"That Crowe Boy..." *Premiere Magazine* July 2000.

"Two Men Plead Not Guilty to Demanding Money from Crowe." *AAP Newsfeed* 26 Mar. 2001.

Vecchiarelli, Lillian. "Russell Crowe's Rock Career Heats Up in Texas." *US Weekly* 21 Aug. 2000. http://www.russellcroweheaven.com/InPrint/USweeklyaug2000.html.

"Veteran Aussie Actor Says Crowe's Win Fantastic." *AAP Newsfeed* 26 Mar. 2001.

Williams, Joe. "Our Man in Hollywood." *St. Louis Post-Dispatch* 27 Mar. 2001.

Williamson, Kevin. "Something to Crowe About." *Sun* [Calgary] 26 Mar. 2001.

Winter, Jessica. "Thus Spake Maximus." *Village Voice*. 30 May 2000.

Zanardo, Lisa. "The Real McCoy." *Go* Dec. 1998.